Mometrix
TEST PREPARATION

TerraNova® NEXT

Grade 5 Reading and Language Test Prep Guide

Written and edited by the Mometrix Test Preparation Team
Printed in the United States of America

TABLE OF CONTENTS

Introduction

Thank you for purchasing this resource! You have made the choice to prepare yourself for a test that could have a huge impact on your future, and this guide is designed to help you be fully ready for test day. Obviously, it's important to have a solid understanding of the test material, but you also need to be prepared for the unique environment and stressors of the test, so that you can perform to the best of your abilities.

For this purpose, the first section that appears in this guide is the **Success Strategies**. We've devoted countless hours to meticulously researching what works and what doesn't, and we've boiled down our findings to the most impactful steps you can take to improve your performance on the test. We start at the beginning with study planning and move through the preparation process, all the way to the testing strategies that will help you get the most out of what you know when you're finally sitting in front of the test.

We recommend that you start preparing for your test as far in advance as possible. However, if you've bought this guide as a last-minute study resource and only have a few days before your test, we recommend that you skip over the first two Success Strategies since they address a long-term study plan.

If you struggle with **test anxiety**, we strongly encourage you to check out our recommendations for how you can overcome it. Test anxiety is a formidable foe, but it can be beaten, and we want to make sure you have the tools you need to defeat it.

Strategy #1 – Plan Big, Study Small

There's a lot riding on your performance. If you want to ace this test, you're going to need to keep your skills sharp and the material fresh in your mind. You need a plan that lets you review everything you need to know while still fitting in your schedule. We'll break this strategy down into three categories.

Information Organization

Start with the information you already have: the official test outline. From this, you can make a complete list of all the concepts you need to cover before the test. Organize these concepts into groups that can be studied together, and create a list of any related vocabulary you need to learn so you can brush up on any difficult terms. You'll want to keep this vocabulary list handy once you actually start studying since you may need to add to it along the way.

Time Management

Once you have your set of study concepts, decide how to spread them out over the time you have left before the test. Break your study plan into small, clear goals so you have a manageable task for each day and know exactly what you're doing. Then just focus on one small step at a time. When you manage your time this way, you don't need to spend hours at a time studying. Studying a small block of content for a short period each day helps you retain information better and avoid stressing over how much you have left to do. You can relax knowing that you have a plan to cover everything in time. In order for this strategy to be effective though, you have to start studying early and stick to your schedule. Avoid the exhaustion and futility that comes from last-minute cramming!

Study Environment

The environment you study in has a big impact on your learning. Studying in a coffee shop, while probably more enjoyable, is not likely to be as fruitful as studying in a quiet room. It's important to keep distractions to a minimum. You're only planning to study for a short block of time, so make the most of it. Don't pause to check your phone or get up to find a snack. It's also important to **avoid multitasking**. Research has consistently shown that multitasking will make your studying dramatically less effective. Your study area should also be comfortable and well-lit so you don't have the distraction of straining your eyes or sitting on an uncomfortable chair.

The time of day you study is also important. You want to be rested and alert. Don't wait until just before bedtime. Study when you'll be most likely to comprehend and remember. Even better, if you know what time of day your test will be, set that time aside for study. That way your brain will be used to working on that subject at that specific time and you'll have a better chance of recalling information.

Finally, it can be helpful to team up with others who are studying for the same test. Your actual studying should be done in as isolated an environment as possible, but the work of organizing the information and setting up the study plan can be divided up. In between study sessions, you can discuss with your teammates the concepts that you're all studying and quiz each other on the details. Just be sure that your teammates are as serious about the test as you are. If you find that your study time is being replaced with social time, you might need to find a new team.

Strategy #2 – Make Your Studying Count

You're devoting a lot of time and effort to preparing for this test, so you want to be absolutely certain it will pay off. This means doing more than just reading the content and hoping you can remember it on test day. It's important to make every minute of study count. There are two main areas you can focus on to make your studying count.

Retention

It doesn't matter how much time you study if you can't remember the material. You need to make sure you are retaining the concepts. To check your retention of the information you're learning, try recalling it at later times with minimal prompting. Try carrying around flashcards and glance at one or two from time to time or ask a friend who's also studying for the test to quiz you.

To enhance your retention, look for ways to put the information into practice so that you can apply it rather than simply recalling it. If you're using the information in practical ways, it will be much easier to remember. Similarly, it helps to solidify a concept in your mind if you're not only reading it to yourself but also explaining it to someone else. Ask a friend to let you teach them about a concept you're a little shaky on (or speak aloud to an imaginary audience if necessary). As you try to summarize, define, give examples, and answer your friend's questions, you'll understand the concepts better and they will stay with you longer. Finally, step back for a big picture view and ask yourself how each piece of information fits with the whole subject. When you link the different concepts together and see them working together as a whole, it's easier to remember the individual components.

Finally, practice showing your work on any multi-step problems, even if you're just studying. Writing out each step you take to solve a problem will help solidify the process in your mind, and you'll be more likely to remember it during the test.

Modality

Modality simply refers to the means or method by which you study. Choosing a study modality that fits your own individual learning style is crucial. No two people learn best in exactly the same way, so it's important to know your strengths and use them to your advantage.

For example, if you learn best by visualization, focus on visualizing a concept in your mind and draw an image or a diagram. Try color-coding your notes, illustrating them, or creating symbols that will trigger your mind to recall a learned concept. If you learn best by hearing or discussing information, find a study partner who learns the same way or read aloud to yourself. Think about how to put the information in your own words. Imagine that you are giving a lecture on the topic and record yourself so you can listen to it later.

For any learning style, flashcards can be helpful. Organize the information so you can take advantage of spare moments to review. Underline key words or phrases. Use different colors for different categories. Mnemonic devices (such as creating a short list in which every item starts with the same letter) can also help with retention. Find what works best for you and use it to store the information in your mind most effectively and easily.

Strategy #3 – Practice the Right Way

Your success on test day depends not only on how many hours you put into preparing, but also on whether you prepared the right way. It's good to check along the way to see if your studying is paying off. One of the most effective ways to do this is by taking practice tests to evaluate your progress. Practice tests are useful because they show exactly where you need to improve. Every time you take a practice test, pay special attention to these three groups of questions:

- The questions you got wrong
- The questions you had to guess on, even if you guessed right
- The questions you found difficult or slow to work through

This will show you exactly what your weak areas are, and where you need to devote more study time. Ask yourself why each of these questions gave you trouble. Was it because you didn't understand the material? Was it because you didn't remember the vocabulary? Do you need more repetitions on this type of question to build speed and confidence? Dig into those questions and figure out how you can strengthen your weak areas as you go back to review the material.

Additionally, many practice tests have a section explaining the answer choices. It can be tempting to read the explanation and think that you now have a good understanding of the concept. However, an explanation likely only covers part of the question's broader context. Even if the explanation makes perfect sense, **go back and investigate** every concept related to the question until you're positive you have a thorough understanding.

As you go along, keep in mind that the practice test is just that: practice. Memorizing these questions and answers will not be very helpful on the actual test because it is unlikely to have any of the same exact questions. If you only know the right answers to the sample questions, you won't be prepared for the real thing. **Study the concepts** until you understand them fully, and then you'll be able to answer any question that shows up on the test.

It's important to wait on the practice tests until you're ready. If you take a test on your first day of study, you may be overwhelmed by the amount of material covered and how much you need to learn. Work up to it gradually.

On test day, you'll need to be prepared for answering questions, managing your time, and using the test-taking strategies you've learned. It's a lot to balance, like a mental marathon that will have a big impact on your future. Like training for a marathon, you'll need to start slowly and work your way up. When test day arrives, you'll be ready.

Start with the strategies you've read in the first two Success Strategies—plan your course and study in the way that works best for you. If you have time, consider using multiple study resources to get different approaches to the same concepts. It can be helpful to see difficult concepts from more than one angle. Then find a good source for practice tests. Many times, the test website will suggest potential study resources or provide sample tests.

Practice Test Strategy

If you're able to find at least three practice tests, we recommend this strategy:

Untimed and Open-Book Practice

Take the first test with no time constraints and with your notes and study guide handy. Take your time and focus on applying the strategies you've learned.

Timed and Open-Book Practice

Take the second practice test open-book as well, but set a timer and practice pacing yourself to finish in time.

Timed and Closed-Book Practice

Take any other practice tests as if it were test day. Set a timer and put away your study materials. Sit at a table or desk in a quiet room, imagine yourself at the testing center, and answer questions as quickly and accurately as possible.

Keep repeating timed and closed-book tests on a regular basis until you run out of practice tests or it's time for the actual test. Your mind will be ready for the schedule and stress of test day, and you'll be able to focus on recalling the material you've learned.

Strategy #4 – Pace Yourself

Once you're fully prepared for the material on the test, your biggest challenge on test day will be managing your time. Just knowing that the clock is ticking can make you panic even if you have plenty of time left. Work on pacing yourself so you can build confidence against the time constraints of the exam. Pacing is a difficult skill to master, especially in a high-pressure environment, so **practice is vital**.

Set time expectations for your pace based on how much time is available. For example, if a section has 60 questions and the time limit is 30 minutes, you know you have to average 30 seconds or less per question in order to answer them all. Although 30 seconds is the hard limit, set 25 seconds per question as your goal, so you reserve extra time to spend on harder questions. When you budget extra time for the harder questions, you no longer have any reason to stress when those questions take longer to answer.

Don't let this time expectation distract you from working through the test at a calm, steady pace, but keep it in mind so you don't spend too much time on any one question. Recognize that taking extra time on one question you don't understand may keep you from answering two that you do understand later in the test. If your time limit for a question is up and you're still not sure of the answer, mark it and move on, and come back to it later if the time and the test format allow. If the testing format doesn't allow you to return to earlier questions, just make an educated guess; then put it out of your mind and move on.

On the easier questions, be careful not to rush. It may seem wise to hurry through them so you have more time for the challenging ones, but it's not worth missing one if you know the concept and just didn't take the time to read the question fully. Work efficiently but make sure you understand the question and have looked at all of the answer choices, since more than one may seem right at first.

Even if you're paying attention to the time, you may find yourself a little behind at some point. You should speed up to get back on track, but do so wisely. Don't panic; just take a few seconds less on each question until you're caught up. Don't guess without thinking, but do look through the answer choices and eliminate any you know are wrong. If you can get down to two choices, it is often worthwhile to guess from those. Once you've chosen an answer, move on and don't dwell on any that you skipped or had to hurry through. If a question was taking too long, chances are it was one of the harder ones, so you weren't as likely to get it right anyway.

On the other hand, if you find yourself getting ahead of schedule, it may be beneficial to slow down a little. The more quickly you work, the more likely you are to make a careless mistake that will affect your score. You've budgeted time for each question, so don't be afraid to spend that time. Practice an efficient but careful pace to get the most out of the time you have.

Test-Taking Strategies

This section contains a list of test-taking strategies that you may find helpful as you work through the test. By taking what you know and applying logical thought, you can maximize your chances of answering any question correctly!

It is very important to realize that every question is different and every person is different: no single strategy will work on every question, and no single strategy will work for every person. That's why we've included all of them here, so you can try them out and determine which ones work best for different types of questions and which ones work best for you.

Question Strategies

⊘ Read Carefully

Read the question and the answer choices carefully. Don't miss the question because you misread the terms. You have plenty of time to read each question thoroughly and make sure you understand what is being asked. Yet a happy medium must be attained, so don't waste too much time. You must read carefully and efficiently.

⊘ Contextual Clues

Look for contextual clues. If the question includes a word you are not familiar with, look at the immediate context for some indication of what the word might mean. Contextual clues can often give you all the information you need to decipher the meaning of an unfamiliar word. Even if you can't determine the meaning, you may be able to narrow down the possibilities enough to make a solid guess at the answer to the question.

⊘ Prefixes

If you're having trouble with a word in the question or answer choices, try dissecting it. Take advantage of every clue that the word might include. Prefixes can be a huge help. Usually, they allow you to determine a basic meaning. *Pre-* means before, *post-* means after, *pro-* is positive, *de-* is negative. From prefixes, you can get an idea of the general meaning of the word and try to put it into context.

⊘ Hedge Words

Watch out for critical hedge words, such as *likely, may, can, often, almost, mostly, usually, generally, rarely,* and *sometimes.* Question writers insert these hedge phrases to cover every possibility. Often an answer choice will be wrong simply because it leaves no room for exception. Be on guard for answer choices that have definitive words such as *exactly* and *always.*

⊘ Switchback Words

Stay alert for *switchbacks.* These are the words and phrases frequently used to alert you to shifts in thought. The most common switchback words are *but, although,* and *however.* Others include *nevertheless, on the other hand, even though, while, in spite of, despite,* and *regardless of.* Switchback words are important to catch because they can change the direction of the question or an answer choice.

✓ Face Value

When in doubt, use common sense. Accept the situation in the problem at face value. Don't read too much into it. These problems will not require you to make wild assumptions. If you have to go beyond creativity and warp time or space in order to have an answer choice fit the question, then you should move on and consider the other answer choices. These are normal problems rooted in reality. The applicable relationship or explanation may not be readily apparent, but it is there for you to figure out. Use your common sense to interpret anything that isn't clear.

Answer Choice Strategies

✓ Answer Selection

The most thorough way to pick an answer choice is to identify and eliminate wrong answers until only one is left, then confirm it is the correct answer. Sometimes an answer choice may immediately seem right, but be careful. The test writers will usually put more than one reasonable answer choice on each question, so take a second to read all of them and make sure that the other choices are not equally obvious. As long as you have time left, it is better to read every answer choice than to pick the first one that looks right without checking the others.

✓ Answer Choice Families

An answer choice family consists of two (in rare cases, three) answer choices that are very similar in construction and cannot all be true at the same time. If you see two answer choices that are direct opposites or parallels, one of them is usually the correct answer. For instance, if one answer choice says that quantity *x* increases and another either says that quantity *x* decreases (opposite) or says that quantity *y* increases (parallel), then those answer choices would fall into the same family. An answer choice that doesn't match the construction of the answer choice family is more likely to be incorrect. Most questions will not have answer choice families, but when they do appear, you should be prepared to recognize them.

✓ Eliminate Answers

Eliminate answer choices as soon as you realize they are wrong, but make sure you consider all possibilities. If you are eliminating answer choices and realize that the last one you are left with is also wrong, don't panic. Start over and consider each choice again. There may be something you missed the first time that you will realize on the second pass.

✓ Avoid Fact Traps

Don't be distracted by an answer choice that is factually true but doesn't answer the question. You are looking for the choice that answers the question. Stay focused on what the question is asking for so you don't accidentally pick an answer that is true but incorrect. Always go back to the question and make sure the answer choice you've selected actually answers the question and is not merely a true statement.

✓ Extreme Statements

In general, you should avoid answers that put forth extreme actions as standard practice or proclaim controversial ideas as established fact. An answer choice that states the "process should be used in certain situations, if..." is much more likely to be correct than one that states the "process should be discontinued completely." The first is a calm rational statement and doesn't even make a definitive, uncompromising stance, using a hedge word *if* to provide wiggle room, whereas the second choice is far more extreme.

⊘ Benchmark

As you read through the answer choices and you come across one that seems to answer the question well, mentally select that answer choice. This is not your final answer, but it's the one that will help you evaluate the other answer choices. The one that you selected is your benchmark or standard for judging each of the other answer choices. Every other answer choice must be compared to your benchmark. That choice is correct until proven otherwise by another answer choice beating it. If you find a better answer, then that one becomes your new benchmark. Once you've decided that no other choice answers the question as well as your benchmark, you have your final answer.

⊘ Predict the Answer

Before you even start looking at the answer choices, it is often best to try to predict the answer. When you come up with the answer on your own, it is easier to avoid distractions and traps because you will know exactly what to look for. The right answer choice is unlikely to be word-for-word what you came up with, but it should be a close match. Even if you are confident that you have the right answer, you should still take the time to read each option before moving on.

General Strategies

⊘ Tough Questions

If you are stumped on a problem or it appears too hard or too difficult, don't waste time. Move on! Remember though, if you can quickly check for obviously incorrect answer choices, your chances of guessing correctly are greatly improved. Before you completely give up, at least try to knock out a couple of possible answers. Eliminate what you can and then guess at the remaining answer choices before moving on.

⊘ Check Your Work

Since you will probably not know every term listed and the answer to every question, it is important that you get credit for the ones that you do know. Don't miss any questions through careless mistakes. If at all possible, try to take a second to look back over your answer selection and make sure you've selected the correct answer choice and haven't made a costly careless mistake (such as marking an answer choice that you didn't mean to mark). This quick double check should more than pay for itself in caught mistakes for the time it costs.

⊘ Pace Yourself

It's easy to be overwhelmed when you're looking at a page full of questions; your mind is confused and full of random thoughts, and the clock is ticking down faster than you would like. Calm down and maintain the pace that you have set for yourself. Especially as you get down to the last few minutes of the test, don't let the small numbers on the clock make you panic. As long as you are on track by monitoring your pace, you are guaranteed to have time for each question.

⊘ Don't Rush

It is very easy to make errors when you are in a hurry. Maintaining a fast pace in answering questions is pointless if it makes you miss questions that you would have gotten right otherwise. Test writers like to include distracting information and wrong answers that seem right. Taking a little extra time to avoid careless mistakes can make all the difference in your test score. Find a pace that allows you to be confident in the answers that you select.

⊘ KEEP MOVING

Panicking will not help you pass the test, so do your best to stay calm and keep moving. Taking deep breaths and going through the answer elimination steps you practiced can help to break through a stress barrier and keep your pace.

Final Notes

The combination of a solid foundation of content knowledge and the confidence that comes from practicing your plan for applying that knowledge is the key to maximizing your performance on test day. As your foundation of content knowledge is built up and strengthened, you'll find that the strategies included in this chapter become more and more effective in helping you quickly sift through the distractions and traps of the test to isolate the correct answer.

Now that you're preparing to move forward into the test content chapters of this book, be sure to keep your goal in mind. As you read, think about how you will be able to apply this information on the test. If you've already seen sample questions for the test and you have an idea of the question format and style, try to come up with questions of your own that you can answer based on what you're reading. This will give you valuable practice applying your knowledge in the same ways you can expect to on test day.

Good luck and good studying!

Reading Language Arts

Comprehension Skills

Generating Questions About Texts Before, During, and After Reading

Asking questions during the process of reading is one way for you to become a more **active reader**. Active readers do not just sit back and have the content handed to them. Instead, they get involved with the text and are part of the process of learning. Asking questions before you read, pausing to ask questions while you're reading, and asking questions after you read are all good ways to help you become a more active reader. There are three types of questioning that can use as you try to think of questions.

Questioning Yourself

These are questions you ask yourself to see how well you're paying attention, and how involved you are in the story. Some example questions are

- Which character is my favorite so far?
- What do I think is going to happen next?
- Is there a character I am similar to in this story? Do I like those similarities?
- What would I do if I was in this situation?

Questioning the Author

Although the chances are slim that you will ever get the chance to meet most of the authors of the texts you read, another way to get involved in the text is to imagine that you are asking questions of the author him or herself. Some example questions are

- What did the author want me to see here?
- Why did he write about this subject?
- Why did the author use this phrase?
- What did she want the character to learn from this?

Questioning the Text

The last type of question you can ask to improve your reading is called questioning the text. To ask these questions, imagine that you are asking the text itself questions about how it works and what it means. Some examples are:

- What does this word mean?
- What is this paragraph describing?
- Why is this term used here?
- How does this sentence connect to the other sentences in this paragraph?

Predicting What Will Happen in a Story

When you read a story, you should look for clues to make a prediction about what will happen. At the end of the story, you may even think about what will happen next to the main character, and use the clues in the story to make a prediction. You can also use personal experience to help make a prediction.

Suppose there is a story about a boy going swimming, and he swims too far out. Suppose the story says the boy can't get back to shore and starts to yell. Suppose the lifeguard comes and helps him. Suppose the story stops after the boy goes back in the water again. The reader might make the prediction that the boy won't swim as far out this time. This may not be true, but it is the most likely thing to happen.

Example

Describe what prediction can be made based on the following sentences:

> When Glen is sick, his mother keeps him home from school. He stays in bed all day and takes medicine. Glen woke up this morning with a sore throat. His head was hot, and he felt achy.

The story says that Glen's mother keeps him home when he is sick and that Glen spends the day in bed when he is sick. The story says that Glen woke up this morning with a sore throat. His head was hot, and he felt achy. The reader can figure out that Glen was sick. Because Glen's mother always keeps him home when he is sick, the reader can predict that Glen will be staying home from school and spending the day in bed.

You can also use text features find information to make predictions and verify conclusions determined about different texts. Using key words as clues, looking for bold print words, looking for sentences that include captions, and words that are written in italics are a few features that can be used to help understand and make predictions about a text.

Using Structure and Genre to Make Predictions

The structure and genre of a story can also help readers make predictions. Most stories follow the same structure. They have an exposition, rising action, a climax, falling action, and a resolution. Because most stories follow this structure, readers can predict that each of these parts will occur in the story. For example, rising action usually begins after the conflict of the story is introduced. This means that if characters have not faced any conflict, the reader can predict that something will go wrong for the characters. Likewise, stories in the same genre may contain similar events. For example, in a mystery, the characters work to solve a crime or explain a strange event. So, when reading a mystery, the reader can predict that the conflict will be a crime or event that the characters must learn more about.

Making Connections to Enhance Comprehension

Reading involves thinking. For good comprehension, readers make text-to-self, text-to-text, and text-to-world connections. Making connections helps readers understand text better and predict what might occur next based on what they already know, such as how characters in the story feel or what happened in another text. Readers can make connections before, during, and after reading. Venn diagrams and other graphic organizers can help readers visualize connections.

Text-to-Self

Reading while looking for connections with the reader's life and experiences makes literature more personally relevant and meaningful to readers. Sentences showing text-to-self connections may begin with these examples

- This reminds me of a time when...
- I understand how the character feels because...
- The setting makes me think of...
- I experienced this same thing when...

Text-to-Text

Reading while looking for connections to other texts helps the reader learn to identify the way authors use genre, setting, characters, plot elements, literary structure and devices, and themes to create meaning. Sentences showing text-to-text connections may begin with these examples

- The character in this story reminds me of the character in...
- These two stories are alike because...
- The conflict in this story is similar to the conflict in...
- The relationship between the friends in this story is different than the relationship in...

Text-to-World

Reading while looking for connections to the world helps the reader begin to see literature as a reflection of real life and notice patterns in history and current events. Sentences showing text-to-world connections may begin with these examples

- The event in this story sounds like the event in history when...
- The actions of this character sound like...
- This is like what happened in real life when...
- I heard about this on the news when...

Making Inferences

An **inference** is a **conclusion** or generalization that the reader makes based on the information provided within a text. Certain facts are included to help a reader come to a specific conclusion.

For example, a story may open with a man trudging through the snow on a cold winter day, dragging a sled behind him. The reader can infer from the setting of the story that the man is wearing heavy winter clothes in order to stay warm. Information is implied based on the setting of a story, which is why setting is an important element of the text. If the same man in the example was trudging down a beach on a hot summer day, dragging a surf board behind him, the reader would assume that the man is not wearing heavy clothes. The reader makes inferences based on their own experiences and the information presented to them in the story.

Readers may come to their own conclusion about a topic, or the author may state a conclusion at the end of a story. When readers are in the middle of a story, they can predict what will happen at the end of it based on the events that have occurred so far and the typical characteristics that have been presented by the author up to that point. A reader needs to consider all of the information that an author has presented, including the main point and supporting points, to make logical conclusions and inferences about the story.

Sometimes interpreting the information in a sentence can be difficult, especially if the reader is unfamiliar with some of the words used in a sentence. Drawing a picture of what is actually happening in the sentence can help, along with looking at the words that the reader does understand in the sentence. By taking a pen or pencil and underlining important information in a sentence, the reader can better understand what the author is trying to say and draw a clearer conclusion from that. Using context clues, or wording in a sentence, is an important way to identify what the author is talking about in the story. An author will often leave blanks for the reader to fill in on their own, using information that has been presented up to that point in the story.

Example

Describe what can be inferred from the following sentences:

> Sometimes after a big storm, the beaches are covered with dead fish, seaweed, broken shells, and pieces of wood. Most seaweed is brown or gold, but there are often pieces of white seaweed. If people visit the beaches, the white seaweed disappears very quickly. It makes a delicious pudding.

To make an inference a reader needs to look for clues in a text. The author does not tell an inference directly; the author hints at one. Here the text says that fish, seaweed, and shells are on the beach after a storm. It also says that some of the seaweed is white and adds that the white seaweed is used for pudding. Another clue is that the white seaweed disappears quickly if people visit the beaches. The inference that a reader can figure out is that the people take the seaweed. It disappears quickly because it can be used to make a delicious pudding.

Example

Read the following two sentences and draw a conclusion based on the text:

> Sarah worked hard on her science project. Her presentation of the science project to the class went well.

Based on the two sentences, the reader can conclude that Sarah will receive a high grade on her science project. The reader knows that Sarah put a great deal of time and effort into her project and that the actual presentation of the project was successful. Based on these facts, the reader can assume that the teacher will appreciate and reward Sarah's effort. This conclusion can be drawn based on the reader's knowledge of how high grades are obtained and their own previous experience with school projects. The reader can assume that Sarah's assessment of her presentation is accurate, that the presentation did indeed conform to high expectations. When a conclusion is drawn based on information the reader is given in a text, the conclusion is called an *inference.*

Example

Read the following sentence. Draw a conclusion based upon the information presented.

> "A rosy-faced servant-maid opened the door, and smiled as she took the letter which he silently offered."

The reader can conclude, based on the sentence, that the servant-maid is friendly. The words "rosy-faced" and "smiled" lead the reader to this conclusion. People who are friendly are often described as having rosy complexions and smiling as a common sign of pleasantness. The reader can also assume, from the sentence, that the letter does not present any threat or unpleasantness to the servant-maid. The person presenting the letter does not have anything to say upon offering it, so perhaps he is waiting to see how the servant-maid will react.

When interpreting a sentence, always look for key words that describe a character. The author carefully crafts a description of each character, to form a picture in the reader's mind about what the character is like.

Key Ideas and Supporting Details

Identifying **key ideas** helps the reader see what a text or story is mostly about. They are the **most important ideas** in a text, and everything else in the text builds around and supports them. Every piece of writing has key ideas. The **supporting details** in a story, such as the characters, events, and settings, will work together to reveal the key ideas. The details are not key ideas, themselves. They make the key ideas clear and show the reader the author's purpose for writing the text.

SYNTHESIZING A TEXT WITH EXISTING KNOWLEDGE

Synthesizing is similar to summarizing but it takes it one step further. Synthesizing involves taking the main points of a text and comparing it with existing knowledge to create a new idea, perspective, or way of thinking.

EXAMPLE

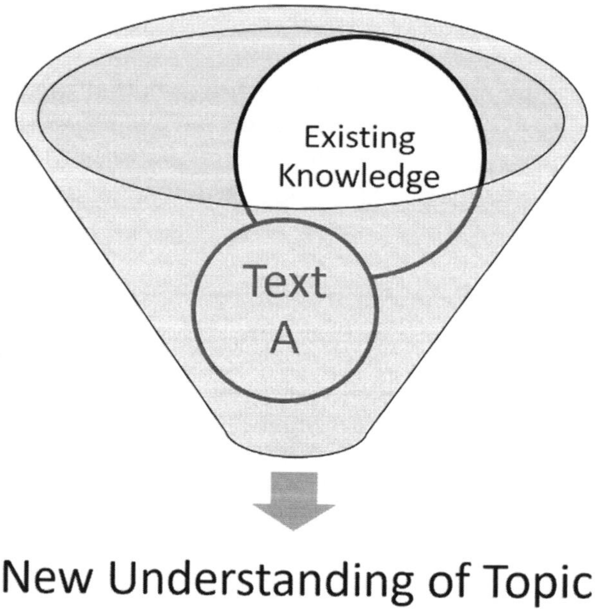

Another term for knowledge that you already have is **schema**. The plural form of this word is **schemata**. Schemata contain all the ideas you have about something. Synthesizing is all about how schemata change over time with the introduction of new information.

Using self-questioning strategies can help readers synthesize texts with their schemata to increase or change their understanding of topics. These questions include

- What do I already know about this topic?
- Is any of this new information?
- Has my perspective changed now that I've read this?
- What do I understand now that I didn't before?
- What are the main ideas of this text?
- How do the parts of the text fit together to create meaning?
- Are there any text-to-text, text-to-self, or text-to-world connections here?

SYNTHESIZING TEXTS WITHOUT EXISTING KNOWLEDGE

If the reader is completely unfamiliar with the topic, they will have no background knowledge. In this case, instead of using existing knowledge, synthesizing may instead be done by combining the ideas provided in two or three different texts. The reader must make connections between the texts, determine how the ideas fit together, and gather evidence to support the new perspective.

Chapter Quiz

1. There are three types of questioning that you can use for active reading. What are these three types of questions?

a. Questioning the composition, grammar, and style of the writing
b. Questioning history, current events, and the future
c. Questioning your personal context, surrounding culture, and the world
d. Questioning yourself, the author, and the text

2. Which of the following helps the reader learn to identify ways authors use genre, setting, characters, plot elements, literary structure and devices, and themes to create meaning?

a. Reading while looking for connections to the reader's life
b. Reading while looking for connections to other texts
c. Reading while looking for connections to the world
d. Reading while looking for connections to history

3. Which of the following is a conclusion that the reader makes using clues in the text?

a. Thesis
b. Prediction
c. Inference
d. Guess

4. What term refers to knowledge that you already have?

a. Cognition
b. Glossary
c. Schema
d. Explicit information

Chapter Quiz Answer Key

1. D: See section **Generating Questions About Texts Before, During, and After Reading**

2. B: See section **Making Connections to Enhance Comprehension**

3. C: See section **Making Inferences**

4. C: See section **Synthesizing a Text with Existing Knowledge**

Response Skills

Text Evidence

The term **text evidence** refers to information found in a text that supports a reader's claim about the text. A reader can draw conclusions or inferences based upon information found in a text. Often, the author will deliberately include information that supports the main point of the text to help the reader make conclusions and inferences that align with the author's purpose for writing the text.

Drawing Conclusions Based on Text Evidence

Readers often need to use prior experience and background information to draw an accurate conclusion about the passage they are reading. Sometimes interpreting the information in a sentence can be difficult, especially if the reader is unfamiliar with some of the words used in a sentence. Looking at the words that the reader does understand in the sentence can help. By taking a pen or pencil and underlining important information in a sentence, the reader can better understand what the author is trying to say and draw a clearer conclusion from that.

Example

Draw a conclusion based on the following quote from *Flora & Ulysses: The Illuminated Adventures* by Kate DiCamillo

> Take this squirrel, for instance. Ulysses. Do I believe he can type poetry? Sure, I do believe it. There is much more beauty in the world if I believe such a thing is possible.

This quote is from the character Dr. Meescham, who is speaking to Flora about her squirrel, Ulysses. Saying a squirrel can type seems silly, but the doctor says he does believe it's true. The phrase "there is much more beauty... if I believe" helps the reader draw the conclusion that Dr. Meescham encourages imagination, and that seeing the world as beautiful is important. The things characters say often show something important about them. Be sure to read dialogue carefully to see what conclusions the author might be wanting you to make.

Example

Read the following quote from *Shiloh* by Phyliss Reynolds Naylor and draw a conclusion based upon the information presented.

> Last of all, I take the lard bread from my pocket and feed it to Shiloh in little pieces, letting him lick my fingers after every bite. I wrap my arms around him, pat him, run my hands over his ears, even kiss his nose. I tell him about a million times I love him as much as I love my ma.

The reader can conclude that the narrator adores his dog Shiloh. The words "wrap my arms around him," "kiss his nose," and "tell him about a million times I love him" lead the reader to this conclusion. The reader can also assume that Shiloh loves the narrator as well because he allows all of the touches that he is receiving. Readers know from experience that animals do not often allow touch from people they do not have affection for.

When interpreting a sentence, always look for key phrases that can be used to draw conclusions about characters and their relationships. Authors carefully craft descriptions of each character to form a picture in the reader's mind about what the character is like.

Paraphrasing and Summarizing

Paraphrasing and summarizing are two ways readers can work to understand what they read. Both involve reading a text and recalling the main points in an accurate way, but they differ in several ways.

How to Paraphrase	How to Summarize
State the message in the text in the reader's own words, while keeping the original meaning of the text Take all of the original ideas and word them in a way that the reader can better understand Put what the reader has read into their own words, rephrasing what the author has written	State main points of the text clearly and to-the-point. Take information and state it simply, in a much shorter form. Put information in a short form that keeps the main points of the whole text. Do not include many details, just the main idea of the text

Paraphrasing is often done for individual ideas, while summarizing is done for an entire block of text or ideas. Often times, a summary can be done in just one sentence, boiling down the author's words into just main idea.

Review Video: Summarizing Text
Visit mometrix.com/academy and enter code: 172903

Paraphrasing the Main Point of a Sentence

Paraphrase the main point of the following two sentences:

> Emmanuel went swimming in the lake by his house, where the water reached a depth of twenty feet in the middle. He did not venture out more than six feet into the water, however.

When paraphrasing a couple sentences or an entire paragraph, always include the main point of the text being reviewed, this is what the reader needs to know about the text. In the example, the reader needs to know that Emmanuel went swimming in the lake, but not more than six feet out. A paraphrase of the text may include: Emmanuel went swimming six feet out in the lake by his house. That is the main point that the audience needs to know.

Recall that a paraphrase is stating the author's ideas in the reader's own words. A summary typically involves including the main points of a longer text, such as a novel or full story.

Example

Read the following paragraph and then give a one sentence summary statement:

> When choosing a pet, people need to think about what type of home they can offer the animal. For example, a small apartment might not be a good fit for a large dog, but could be a comfortable home for a kitten. A house that has a big yard would be great for a puppy, but a rabbit does not need a large yard.

In order to summarize, one has to identify the main idea and any supporting ideas in the author's work. The summary is an overview of the author's paragraph and will tell what it is about without getting into any of the details. The summary needs to be broad enough to cover all of the information in the author's paragraph. Here is a possible summary statement for the above paragraph:

People need to consider a number of factors when choosing a pet.

Example

Read the following sentences and then paraphrase the material:

> The government is debating a new health care system for our country. The Senate and the House of Representatives have both passed bills; now they need to resolve these two bills into one bill that a majority can agree on.

When paraphrasing information, one needs to read carefully and pay attention to details, then put the material away and write or tell it in their own words. One does not want to look at the material while paraphrasing to avoid plagiarizing by accident. Here is one example of a way to paraphrase the sentences:

> Our government is trying to adopt a new health care system. The Senate has passed a bill and so has the House of Representatives. Their bills are different so now they have to compromise on one bill that can be passed.

Chapter Quiz

1. If a reader takes an author's original idea and then restates it, putting the idea into their own words, this is an example of:

a. Outlining text
b. Paraphrasing text
c. Summarizing text
d. Abstracting text

2. Which of the following is NOT true of summarizing?

a. A summary can be just one sentence that boils down the author's words into the main idea.
b. Summarizing helps readers work to understand what they have read.
c. A summary typically involves restating the main points of a text in a simpler, shorter fashion.
d. A summary should be subjective and include brief personal opinions on the subject.

Chapter Quiz Answer Key

1. B: See section **Paraphrasing and Summarizing**

2. D: See section **Paraphrasing and Summarizing**

Literary Elements

THEME

The **theme** of a story, essay, or poem is the lesson that it teaches, or the message the author wants to get across. The theme is linked to the characters, the setting, and the events in a story. A passage can have two or more themes that convey its overall idea.

The theme of a story is not the same as the topic of a story. The topic is what the story is about, but the theme is what a reader is meant to learn. When readers are discussing theme, they can determine both theme topics as well as theme statements.

Theme topics are broad ideas that apply to the text. Examples are:

- Love
- The importance of friendship
- Good vs. evil
- The circle of life

Themes may also be complete statements written in sentence form. Examples are:

- Acts of courage can bring positive changes to the world.
- True friendship can withstand the hardest challenges.

Some themes are fairly common. These themes are called **universal themes** and they suggest things about life, society, and human nature.

Themes are very rarely stated in the text. Instead, the reader has to **infer** the theme by reading closely and thinking carefully about what the author is saying.

Themes are an important part of literature because they serve the purpose of teaching the reader or listener a truth about life. The theme is developed by how a character or characters respond to their situations and challenges.

EXAMPLE

Read the following and consider the theme of the excerpt.

> Jeanie arrived at the bake sale early. She bought the biggest cake at the sale. Sally had to work late. When she finally got to the sale, no cakes were left. She got only two cookies. She was lucky to get anything.

The saying "the early bird gets the worm" is one way to explain the theme of the story. In the story we read that Jeanie arrived early at the bake sale and got the biggest cake. But when Sally arrived, all that was left were two cookies. The point of the story is that the early bird gets the worm—the worm in this case is a large cake.

Characters

Character Trait

The traits of a character may include how they act and physical characteristics; a character trait is a behavior or physical characteristic that is unique to a specific character. For example, a character may be outgoing, which means he or she likes to talk a lot, or they may have bright red hair. These are both character traits.

An author uses character traits to describe a character in a story and help the reader to learn more about how the character acts and what they look like. By comparing the character traits in a story, the reader can see similarities and differences between characters. The author includes character traits to help the reader understand why a character may act a certain way in the story. For example, a character who is shy may not want to talk with a lot of people in a new classroom, but a character who is outgoing may want to talk with many people.

An author typically provides many details about a character so that the reader can learn more about the character's traits, motivations, relationships, and any conflicts they may have in the story. The traits of a character may include how they act and how they look. Characters are often motivated by things that have already happened in their life or how they feel about a topic. The author will often give the reader enough information about the character so that the reader can figure out why the character responds to a situation in a certain way. The author will also often give details about the relationships between characters and points they may conflict on. For example, a character may be good friends with another character; however, the two characters may disagree on where to play outside if one character likes being near the water and the other character does not.

Example

Read the following description of a character and decide, logically, whether the character is likely to go hiking outdoors:

> Jeremy lived in a high-rise in Chicago. He was studious, and not very athletic. Jeremy preferred to stay indoors and read a book, rather than enjoy outdoor weather.

Based on the description of the character's traits, preferences, and personality, he is not likely to go hiking outdoors. The description indicates that the character prefers reading, rather than enjoying outdoor weather. In addition, the character lives in a tall building in the middle of a large city, in order for him to enjoy the outdoors, he would have to travel away from where he lives. The character is not likely to change his preferences. A situation may lead the character to go hiking, but he is not likely to initiate the action on his own. A description of a character that is likely to go hiking outdoors may include a preference for outdoor activity and living near trails.

Character Relationships

A relationship is the way one character acts with another character in a story. The characters are often called **major characters** if they have a main part in the story and **minor characters** if they have a smaller part. There are many different kinds of relationships. For example, two children in a story may be friends, but they could be angry with each other, competing with each other, or helping each other. An author may tell the reader what kind of relationship the characters have. An author might give hints about a relationship. For example, the author may show one child making fun of the other child, which would suggest that the two children do not have a friendly relationship. The author might show one child teaching the other child how to read, which would suggest that the two children have a friendly relationship.

Example

Read the following sentences and describe the relationship Jill and Anna have:

> Jill came over to Anna and asked if she wanted an apple. "Sure, I'd love one. Thanks," Anna answered. Anna took a bite of the apple and started to chew it. Her chewing was so loud that they both started to laugh.

The author does not tell what the relationship between Jill and Anna is. The reader must figure it out from their actions. These actions are the clues the author gives. Jill asks Anna if she wants an apple. Anna says yes and starts to eat it. Her chewing is very loud. Both Jill and Anna start to laugh. They seem to like each other. Jill seems generous to Anna because she gives Anna an apple. They laugh together, and friends often laugh together. The reader can use personal experience to decide that it seems as though Jill and Anna are friends.

Character Changes

Characters can change in a multitude of ways throughout a story; however, there are main aspects of a character that change. A character's identifying **characteristics**, such as personality or behavior traits, may change as the result of a prominent event in the story, current **motivations**, and **conflicts**. As conflicts change or are resolved, a character may no longer be motivated by striving toward a goal that was previously important to them. As the plot of a story moves along, characters can constantly change in relation to events that occur. **Relationships** between characters and the points of view of characters may change throughout a story as well.

Each story will have many different types of characters and each of these characters will have a different relationship with other characters. Stories usually have a protagonist, antagonist, and a variety of other characters including round, flat, and stock characters.

Protagonist

The main character in a drama, movie, novel, or other fictional text. The author portrays the protagonist in a way that the audience is most like to identify with themselves. The protagonist is generally undertaking some type of personal challenge throughout the story. The author writes the story so that the reader becomes aware of the protagonist's emotions and is generally able to empathize with the personal challenge.

Antagonist

The character that actively opposes the protagonist by trying to prevent them from succeeding. The antagonist is usually presented in such a way as to make the audience dislike them, and want them to fail at stopping the protagonist. The protagonist and antagonist oppose each other, so their relationship is almost always one of dislike.

Flat Characters

Does not have any substantial changes throughout the story. They stay the same despite the conflict, and do not learn any lessons. They are usually minor characters that might interact with the main character in some way.

Round Characters

Major characters in the story that will be more fully developed than other minor characters. They will usually encounter some type of conflict that they must overcome, and usually learn a lesson about life or themselves along the way.

Stock Characters

Often get their characteristics and mannerisms from stereotypes of people that are widely recognized. These types of characters are often repeated and well-known. Readers should be aware that stereotypes are rarely accurate in reality, and are generally intended to be humorous or dramatic. Some examples are evil stepmothers, unintelligent blondes, rude athletes, and loyal servants.

Plot

The term **plot** refers to the series of events that take place in a story. The events in a story may take place in one location or many, in a short amount of time or over many years. A story always has to start somewhere, and the first event in a story signals the beginning of the plot. Stories may vary in length from half a page to novel-length, but they all follow a progression of events that the author winds together to form the plot. The characters and events in the story determine what the plot will be. Readers may find a **plot line** useful as they try to put the events in the text in order and determine the relationships between events.

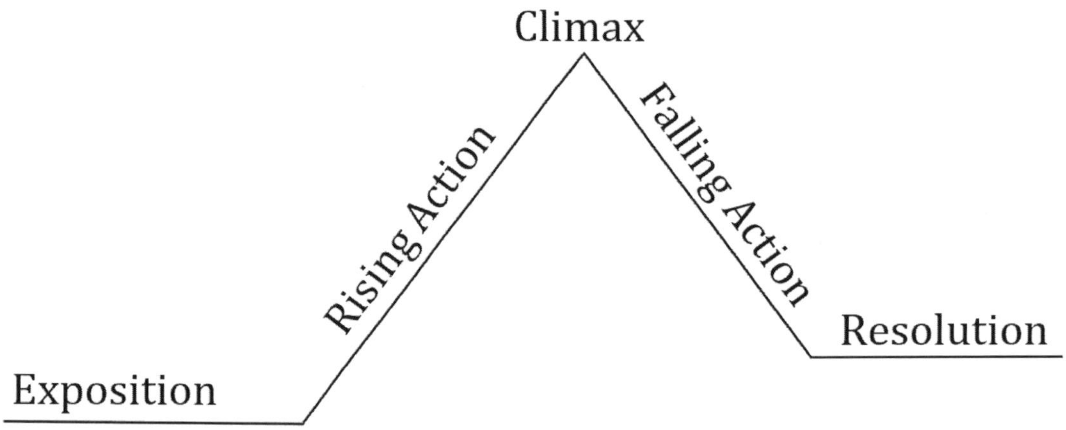

Review Video: Plot Line
Visit mometrix.com/academy and enter code: 944011

Every plot will begin with **exposition**, which introduces the characters and the setting of the story. The plot will continue to develop as new ideas and events centered on the main conflict in the story are revealed, which is called the **rising action**. The action in the story will rise until a **climax** is reached within the conflict. The climax can also be referred to as the turning point in the story, since the climax is where each character makes an important decision. After the climax, the action starts to wind down during the **falling action**. At this point, the characters begin to follow the paths they chose in during climax. The events of the story reach **resolution** in some way by the end of the story. Some conflicts are left open-ended, so that the reader is left to decide what really happened at the end of the story. Keep in mind that not all resolutions are happy or peaceful.

Example

Read the following plot and determine what the missing event is in the plot sequence:

> Sarita went to the store to buy eggs for her mother. She bought the eggs and got back on her bicycle to bring the eggs home. Her mother was angry that the eggs were all broken.

The reader has to guess based on the plot sequence what happened between events. The reader knows that Sarita got on her bicycle to go home. The reader also knows that the eggs were broken when she arrived at the house. Based on the context, the reader can assume that Sarita fell off her bicycle or dropped the eggs on the way home, causing them to all be broken when she arrived. The reader can assume that Sarita would have noticed if the eggs were already broken in the store. Plot often follows a logical sequence of events, but sometimes it is difficult to decide what actually happened between two events. In the example, the reader can logically assume that the eggs were broken on the way home.

Conflict

Conflict creates the basis for the plot of a story. A conflict may be between characters, a character and their own mind, or an outside influence. The main point of a conflict is that there is a problem that needs to be resolved. The problem may be a disagreement or an obstacle that has arisen and needs to be overcome.

An important part of analyzing the plot of a passage is identifying the **main conflict**. There will likely be many smaller conflicts in the story, but there will be one main problem that influences the characters and events. To identify the main conflict, first look at who the main character is. Now ask yourself what they want. They may want to something to happen or not happen, another character to do or not do something, or to confront or avoid a problem, among other things. Once you know what they want, now ask yourself what is standing in the character's way. It may be a person, an event, or something less tangible like the passing of time. Combining what the main character wants and why they do not currently have leaves the reader with a summary of the main conflict.

Review Video: Conflict
Visit mometrix.com/academy and enter code: 559550

Example

Read the following sentence and explain the main conflict between the two characters:

> Joe stared angrily at Jamie's retreating back as Jamie raced away down the field with Joe's soccer ball.

The main conflict in the sentence is that Jamie has Joe's soccer ball. There may be additional conflicts between the two characters, but none are evident from the evidence shown in the sentence. In any story, a conflict may be minor and only affect part of the story, or be the main focus, taking an entire story to solve a conflict between characters. In the context of the sentence, it is not clear whether or not the entire story will revolve around Jamie taking Joe's soccer ball.

Resolution

The term **resolution** usually indicates the result of a conflict in a story. Conflict between characters, within a character, or against an external element is necessary in order to have a plot for a story. Without conflict, no events would occur to form the story. A conflict will come to a climax, and then conclude in some way. The resolution of a problem may be open-ended, end tragically, or end in a way that is good for everyone involved. The problem resolution typically occurs near the end of a story, after the climax has happened. A problem may be resolved by the characters involved within the conflict or by an external event; an upcoming resolution may be foreshadowed in the text, or may be completely unexpected by the reader. If the resolution is completely unexpected, it is considered to be a **twist** in the story.

EFFECT OF PLOT ON A STORY'S CHARACTERS

The plot of a story unfolds as each event follows another, shaping the characters as they react to the various events that occur. Some characters are able to resolve their problems by the end of the story, while some characters fail to overcome their predicaments. As characters respond to the events around them, they reveal more and more about their personalities. Some grow and some do not. The reader can use the events of the plot to interpret the meaning of the story and understand its characters.

EXAMPLE

Read the excerpt and explain how finding the chest affects Marta.

> The map said this was the spot. Marta held her breath. Her fists were clenched into two tight balls. She lifted the shovel and scooped more sand out of the hole. There it was; she had found the chest with the diamonds. She opened the top. She would never need to work again. She smiled. It was really happening.

The event affects Marta by making her happy. The reader gets several clues that she is anxiously waiting ("Marta held her breath" and "her fists were clenched"), and that she is happy with what she found ("She smiled"). Events can cause characters to have all kinds of feelings. Here, something wonderful happened. However, events in stories are not always quite so happy. For instance, if a robber had suddenly seen Marta and the chest, he might have stolen the chest. That event would have had a very different effect on her. Readers need to pay attention to how characters are reacting to events, whether they are simply hinted at or stated in the story. In this way a reader will learn what characters are like.

SETTING

The setting is where a story **takes place**. The setting of a story may stay the same for the entire story, or change as events in the story unfold. For example, an entire story may take place in one room, or on the other end, a story could cross continents as the reader follows the characters along on a trail of events. Every story has to take place somewhere. The setting of story is described by the author in terms of what it looks like, how the character feels, and anything that is happening at that location at the time. For example, a character may be caught on a doorstep on a cold, rainy day. The character may feel frustrated as he shivers in the doorway, waiting for the heavy rain to let up a bit.

EXAMPLE

When listing ways that a story set in the city has a different backdrop from a story set in the countryside, answers will vary based on current knowledge of common characteristics for each setting. A story set in a city may be different from a story set in the countryside based on the following factors:

- Number of passersby: many people on a sidewalk vs. no other people around
- Background noise: car horns vs. bird calls
- Types of surroundings: tall buildings vs. fields of corn
- Types of transportation: subways and taxis vs. horses and farm trucks

- Daily activities being carried out: sitting at a desk in a skyscraper vs. plowing fields for planting
- Type of attire: a business suit vs. dirty jeans and boots

Shaping a Character with Setting or Plot

The setting of a story shapes character because it helps to define the situation that a character finds herself in. A character is limited to the setting of a story. For example, if a story takes place in a cold environment filled with snow and ice, this is certain to impact what actions a character can and will take. Frequently, the setting changes the way characters behave based on time. For example, the character of a woman who is a single mother in 1920 would be seen and behave very differently than a single mother in 2020.

Example

Read the excerpt and determine how the setting influences the character in this excerpt.

> She had swum too far out. The waves were higher than she thought. She was struggling hard to get to shore. She wondered if she would make it. She thought of her childhood. Had she been right to run away from home, she wondered? Just then, a lifeguard grabbed her and helped her to shore.

The setting of the ocean and the high waves creates a conflict in the character. She is worried. She thinks about her childhood and her parents. She doesn't know if she will make it to shore. This is how the setting affects the character in this excerpt. Without the high waves and the struggle, she would not become so worried and start to think about her past. She probably would not have questioned herself. This is an example of how a setting influences a character. If the waves had not been high, there probably would not have been a struggle or any self-searching of the swimmer's past.

Historical and Cultural Setting

Historical context influences literature in a number of ways. The style of the author's writing can be impacted by the historical period during which it was written (e.g., Dickens wrote at a time when authors were paid by the word; this is why his novels are so long). Obviously, the setting of the book includes its historical context. In addition, dialect may be a function of the historical period of the book. When a reader understands the historical context of a particular book, he or she can have a deeper understanding of the novel. Knowing about the time period during which the author wrote, as well as the time period discussed in the novel, helps the reader understand some of the author's choices, including character motivations.

Patterns Related to Settings

The setting of a story can allow the reader to draw on personal experience about where the story takes place. If a story takes place on a farm, the reader will likely picture a rural, peaceful setting, which may go along with (or be in contrast to) the actual plot of the story. For example, a reader would not expect a scary story to occur on a farm on a sunny day. Conversely, a reader may view a dark subway as a dangerous place, while the plot of a story set there may be based on a very calm series of events. When an author is crafting a story, they need to consider what the audience may already think about a particular setting in order to properly present the events of a story for greatest impact.

Chapter Quiz

1. Which of the following is the lesson that a story teaches, or the message the author wants to get across?

a. Theme
b. Setting
c. Topic
d. Plot

2. What type of character often gets their characteristics and mannerisms from stereotypes of people that are widely recognized?

a. Minor characters
b. Stock characters
c. Flat characters
d. Round characters

3. Every plot will begin with __________, which introduces the characters and the setting of the story.

a. Conflict
b. Rising action
c. Foreshadowing
d. Exposition

4. Which of the following would most likely convey a peaceful setting to the reader?

a. Sunny farm
b. Damp basement
c. Loud construction site
d. Dark subway

Chapter Quiz Answer Key

1. A: See section **Theme**

2. B: See section **Stock Characters**

3. D: See section **Plot**

4. A: See section **Patterns Related to Settings**

Literary Genres

Children's Literature

There are types of texts that are specifically meant to be read by children or younger audiences. Children's literature contains many different **genres**, which are categories that texts can be divided into. Some types of children's literature are

- **Folktales** -Songs, stories, myths, or proverbs belonging to a group of people. Often passed down from generation to generation by word of mouth.
- **Fairy tales** are stories that include fictional creatures or characters with fantastical traits and abilities. Fairy tales often end happily and depict the victory of good over evil. The plots and characters in fairy tales are often far-fetched and whimsical.
- **Fables** –Story told (often by a narrator) full of supernatural features like speaking animals. The tale demonstrates a useful truth at the end.
- **Legends** -A story featuring a national or folk hero. Often has a basis in actual fact, but also contains imaginative material.
- **Myth** -A legend or traditional narrative, often based on a historical event. The story reveals something about human behavior or the natural world, and often involves actions of gods.
- **Tall Tales** -A story full of outlandish exaggerations, often humorous and containing heroes who perform impossible acts easily.

Poetry

Poet Versus Speaker

The author of a poem is called a **poet**. Many poems are written in first person, which means the **stanzas** (groups of lines) include words like "I" and "me." However, the poet is not always the **speaker** of the poem. In a novel, the author can create characters with different points of view. The characters can argue or have different roles to play in telling the story. Similarly, a poet may write a poem from a different point of view or even include more than one voice. The speaker is the voice of the poem, and is not always the same person as the poet him or herself. The reader or listener should know that the person telling the story is a character, and not always a real person.

For example, this excerpt from a poem by Dr. Seuss reads:

> When you think things are bad,
> when you feel sour and blue,
> when you start to get mad...
> you should do what I do!
> Just tell yourself, Duckie,
> you're really quite lucky!
> Some people are much more...
> oh, ever so much more...
> oh, muchly much-much more
> unlucky than you!

Even though one line has the word "I" in it, the poem is not from the perspective of Dr. Seuss. He is the author of the poem, but not the speaker. The person saying "I" is a character, just like in a story.

Sensory Language in Poetry

Sensory language is when the author uses descriptive words and specific details that appeal to a reader's senses (sight, touch, taste, hearing, smell, emotion). For example, the author can use scents that the reader is familiar with to help them imagine what the setting of the poem smells and feels like. This use of sensory language is also called **imagery**.

Rhyme in Poetry

Poets use rhymes to help readers understand poems. Words **rhyme** when they sound similar to each other, especially when the similar sound is at the end of the words, like *cat* and *hat*, or *roar* and *soar*. Rhyming words usually have endings that are spelled the same way, but sometimes they are spelled differently, like *wait* and *hate* or *bear* and *snare*.

Famous poet Shel Silverstein uses rhyme in many of his poems. For example, in his poem "Listen to the Mustn'ts", the last word of the first- and second-lines rhyme with each other, and the last word of the third- and fourth-line rhyme with each other.

> Listen to Mustn'ts, child, listen to the Don'ts.
> Listen to the Shouldn'ts, the Impossibles, the Won'ts.
> Listen to the Never Haves, then listen close to me.
> Anything can happen, child, Anything can be.

The pattern of the rhymes in this poem forms a **rhyme scheme**. Sometimes poets use a rhyme scheme that makes every other line of the poem rhyme instead.

Sound Devices

Sound devices allow authors to add another level to their texts by tapping into the spoken part of language. Authors may use many sound devices to create meaning and help readers understand them better, including:

Onomatopoeia

- Appeals to the reader's sense of hearing by using words that copy the noises objects or people make, like sound effects.
- For example, an author might write "The soccer ball whooshed across the field into the goalie's net, scoring the winning point!" The word "whooshed" is an **onomatopoeia** because it mimics the sound of air moving quickly. Because the writer chose to include an onomatopoeia, the reader is able to better picture the action in the sentence.

Alliteration, Assonance, and Consonance

- Alliteration, assonance, and consonance all deal with using the same sound throughout a line or sentence. **Alliteration** is the use of words that begin with the **same sound** in a sentence or in a line of poetry. **Assonance** refers to alliteration with a repeated **vowel** sound, whereas **consonance** refers to alliteration with **consonant** sounds.
- For example, the following line contains two sets of alliteration: "I saw a fly fly past my eye, straight into a fresh cherry pie. I felt a flea flee away from my knee and onto the sleeping dog." The first line uses the same sound in the words *I, fly, eye,* and *pie,* which is assonance. The second line uses both assonance and consonance, using the same vowel sound in *flea, flee, knee*, and, *sleeping*. The repeated consonants show up in the words *felt, flea*, and *flee.*

> **Review Video: Alliteration in Everyday Expressions**
> Visit mometrix.com/academy and enter code: 462837

Drama

Dramas are texts that are written to be performed by people reading the lines or acting the stories out. They can also be presented as monologues (one character speaks), dialogues (two character speak to each other), or pantomimes (body movements are used instead of spoken words). Dramatic texts are called plays or **scripts**, and they are written differently than other texts.

Text Structure in Drama

Plays are divided into **acts** (large units) and **scenes** (small sections inside acts) instead of chapters. There are also **stage directions**, which are instructions from the playwright about where items go, where actors should move, and what the characters should be doing during the scene. Stage directions are usually in italics to set them apart from other parts of the play. When it is time for a character in a play to speak, there will be **character tag** on the left side of the page which shows the name of the character (all letters of the name are capitalized) followed by a colon.

Here is an example of how a page from a play might look:

Title of Play

Act Number

Scene Number

The setting of the scene is being described here. The reader is being introduced to the characters and the things happening around them. Characters will enter speak to one another during the scene.

CHARACTER 1:
    I am speaking. These are words I say. *(stage directions)* I am still speaking.

    CHARACTER 2 *enters and does something.*

CHARACTER 2:
    Now I am speaking. This is my dialogue.

Dialogue and Stage Directions

Dialogue refers to what the characters say in a play when they are talking to each other, talking to themselves, or even talking to the audience. The type of speech, word choice, and accent a character uses is specific to the role he is playing. For example, a person cast to play a cowboy would have certain words in his vocabulary that a character from a big city in the North would not have.

A playwright also uses stage directions to make the play flow smoothly. Character interaction helps the viewer to understand the mood of the scene. If two characters are confrontational, the viewer is aware that there is some type of conflict occurring. Stage directions create order when all the characters are on stage together.

Informational Text

Controlling Idea

The controlling idea, also called the main idea or thesis, of a passage is usually located in the first paragraph or two of text. Having the controlling idea near the beginning of the passage allows the author to grab the reader's attention and let them know what the rest of the passage will discuss.

To find the controlling idea in a passage, there are questions the reader can ask while reading: What is this passage about? What does the author want the reader to know about the topic? The supporting details will provide evidence that the controlling idea is correct and are found in the body of a passage. The supporting details often provide examples of the controlling idea.

Supporting Details

Provide evidence and backing for the main point. All texts contain details, but they are only classified as supporting details when they serve to reinforce some larger point. Supporting details are most commonly found in informative and persuasive texts. In some cases, they will be clearly indicated with words like **for example** or **for instance**, or they will begin with words like **first**, **second**, and **last**. However, these special words are not a requirement. As a reader, it is important to consider whether the author's supporting details really back up his or her main point. Supporting details can be factual and correct but still not relevant to the author's point. Sometimes, supporting details can seem important but they might not support the main idea in the story well because they are based on opinion that cannot be proven.

Example

Decide whether the following sentence is the main point or a supporting point of a text, and state where the information would be placed in an outline:

> One type of horseback riding, bareback horseback riding, involves sitting on a moving horse without a saddle and grasping the horse's mane.

This sentence is a supporting point, with the main point of the entire text likely about horseback riding in general. As a supporting point, this sentence would go further down in an outline, next to any numeral after numeral I. This sentence can be followed by additional sub-points that further explain the concept of bareback horseback riding. When a supporting point is used to clarify a main point or topic, the supporting point helps to break the topic down into smaller pieces.

Structural Features of Informational Text

Texts which intend to inform the reader about a topic are often accompanied by visual aids or graphics. Some common examples are listed below.

- **Insets and sidebars** show additional information related to the text in boxes or on the sides of the page. Insets can contain pictures or text, and sometimes have different colored backgrounds or font types to make them stand out from the text.
- **Visual aids** include features like diagrams, graphs, and charts. These can help the user think about information in a different way. They do this by visually presenting the relationship between the information in the text.
- **Timelines** are a visual aid which show how events from the text happened over time, and usually contain dates, locations, or other related information.
- **Tables** are visual aids that organize information in a way that shows the relationship between the information. Tables are made using rows and columns, and the pieces in the rows and columns are called cells. Usually, the first row or column will contain a title or heading that categorizes or defines the other cells in that row or column.
- **Bullet points** list items separately, making facts and ideas easier to see and understand.
- **Numbers** can also be used to list separate items. Usually, numbers are used to show that the items are part of a sequence. For example, in a list of instructions, each instruction may be numbered to show the reader the order in which each instruction should be completed.
- **Italics** are a formatting technique that makes text appear slanted. Italics can be used to emphasize text because they cause the text to look different and lead the reader to notice it more easily. Italics are also often used in fiction to show that text is part of a character's thoughts. They are also commonly used to show that a word or section of text is written in a foreign language.
- **Boldface** is a way to format text to make it stand out. Boldface, or bold, text can be used to emphasize a word, phrase, or idea. Boldface can also be used to let the reader know that they can find more information about a term in a glossary, sidebar, or other feature of the text.

Organizational Patterns

Authors want to have an effective text that the reader can understand. If ideas do not follow a **logical order**, the reader will become confused and not know what the author is trying to say. When writing, there are a variety of ways that an author can choose to organize a written work. It is important to choose the pattern that **best presents** the information, as not all patterns will work for every piece of writing. An author may organize ideas according to a timeline, cause and effect, or description of an event or setting.

Order of Importance

The author puts the information in the text in order of what is most important. Order of importance can be either increasing or decreasing, depending on how the writer wants to structure the work.

Chronological Order

The author organizes the progression of events based upon when they occurred and what was included in each step of the story. By organizing the text in this way the author presents all necessary information about the six questions readers can ask to help themselves understand the text: who, what, when, where, why, and how.

Problem and Solution

The author presents some information as a problem and then discusses a solution or attempted solution to that problem. In problem and solution, there is generally one main problem, but that one problem may have several possible solutions.

For example, suppose Billy wants a new video game but does not have the money. There are several possible solutions to this. He might try asking his mom to buy it for him. If that does not work, he could offer to do small jobs to earn enough money to buy it. A third possibility might be to wait until his birthday and ask for it then.

Cause and Effect

The author will write about relationship between two events that occur, where the second event occurs as a result of the first.

For example, a text may discuss a school policy stating that when a student is late to school too many times, they receive a detention. Later in the text, we might see a student repeatedly arriving late to school, after which he is given a detention. In this example, the **cause** is the student being late to school, and the **effect** is the student receiving a detention.

Compare and Contrast

The author will show similarities and differences between items or events.

For example, the author may write about cats and dogs. They might start by giving a brief description of the two. Then they will want to point out all of the similarities, such as; they both have tails, and both are kept as pets. Next, they will explain the differences, such as; dogs are canines, while cats are felines. They will try to provide as much detail as possible about both the similarities and the differences.

Ideas may vary in complexity, in addition to their main point. Topics of debate, or issues, may have pros and cons. By comparing the positive and negative aspects of each view, the reader can better understand how the viewpoints are similar and different.

Example

Read the following two viewpoints and compare and contrast how the two viewpoints are similar and different:

> (1) Basketball is the best sport to play, because a participant can be part of a team and excel individually.
> (2) In basketball, players must work together to execute plays and achieve points for the team.

In the first viewpoint, the author states that basketball is the best sport to play, whereas in the second viewpoint, the author simply states how the game is played. The first viewpoint also refers to an individual player's performance, while the second viewpoint focuses on the fact that the team needs to score points together in order to win the game. The first viewpoint is trying to convince the reader, while the second viewpoint is explaining how the game is played. Yes, an individual may excel at scoring points, as indicated in the first viewpoint, but the second viewpoint emphasizes the fact that plays need to be done together in order to score points for the entire team. Two differing viewpoints will often overlap in relation to the topic that they are discussing.

Identifying Organizational Patterns

Example

Read the following paragraph from a news story and describe how the author organizes information in the story:

> The parade in honor of the town's 200th anniversary began at the corner of 57th Street at 9:00 a.m. on Saturday morning. Members of the fire department led the parade, dressed in their bright red hats and heavy yellow coats. At 9:15 a.m., members of the high school band gave a performance.

The news story uses chronological order organize ideas. The reader is given information about what type of event occurred, when the event occurred, what the event was about, and who was included.

Example

Identify organizational pattern that is used in the following sentence from *Morte d'Arthur* by Sir Thomas Malory:

> The king had given his promise, so he was obliged to agree.

The text structure of cause and effect is used in this sentence. The cause in the sentence is that the king gave his promise, and the effect is that he had to agree.

Argumentative Texts

Identifying the Claim

In a persuasive or argumentative text, the author is writing in order to make and support a claim. A claim is similar to the key idea of an informational text. However, a claim can be argued, which means that some readers may not agree with it. The author of the text will need to use the body of the text to support the claim and show readers why they should agree with it. To identify the claim of a text, first identify the topic. Then, read the introduction text to see what the author writes about the topic.

The claim should be clearly stated in the introduction. However, if the claim is still not clear, read the body to see what kind of evidence the author uses to support the claim. The way that the author gives and applies evidence may also show what the claim of the text is.

Call to Action

Another strategy is to look for a call to action in the text. A call to action is a statement that instructs the reader to do something after reading the text. Often, the call to action will tell the reader to do something that shows that he or she agrees with the author's claim. For example, if an author's claim is that reading is better than watching a movie, the author may include a call to action that says "Turn off the TV and dig in to a new book today!" By including this statement, the author is telling the readers to show their agreement by choosing to read rather than watch a movie.

Identifying How the Author Supports a Claim

In a persuasive or argumentative text, the author must use information to support his or her claim. This information is called evidence. Below are common types of evidence an author may use to support a claim:

- **Facts:** Authors may use facts that show that their claim is true. For example, a claim that fish are better pets than dogs can be supported by the fact that fish cannot make a mess inside a house.

- **Examples:** Authors may give examples of events or experiences that suggest that their claim is true. For example, an author may claim that people should exercise because it will make them healthier. The author could give an example of how exercise can improve a person's health in order to support this claim.
- **Quotes:** An author can support a claim by using quotes from other people or texts. If the person or text makes a statement that shows that the author's claim is true, the author can include that quote in his or her text. When authors include quotes in their work, they must always tell the reader where the quote came from.

The author must use enough evidence to support the claim. If the evidence does not fully support the claim in the text, then the author must continue working to find evidence for the claim. The evidence used to support a claim must also be believable and come from a reliable source.

Identifying the Intended Audience

Authors of persuasive and argumentative texts want to convince others to agree with a claim or take a certain action. Because of this, they will often write to a specific audience. Often, the target audience will include people who disagree with the author's claim. The author's desire is to give these people information that will lead them to change their minds or actions.

Strategies for Identifying the Intended Audience

One way to identify the intended audience of a persuasive or argumentative text is to first identify the author's claim. Then, consider who would disagree with the author's claim. This group of people is likely the group that the author wants to persuade.

Another way to identify the audience is to look for clues in the text. Sometimes, authors will clearly state which people are included in the intended audience. For example, imagine that an author includes the statement, "Teachers should reward their students every time they make a good grade on a test." This shows that the text is written to persuade teachers who do not already reward their students for good test grades. Similarly, a call to action may show who the target audience is by instructing the members of the audience to take a certain action.

Chapter Quiz

1. What type of children's literature can be described as songs, stories, myths, or proverbs belonging to a group of people, that are often passed down from generation to generation by word of mouth?

a. Folktales
b. Fables
c. Legends
d. Tall tales

2. In poetry, which of the following appeals to the reader's sense of hearing by using words that begin with the same consonant sound in a sentence or in a line of poetry?

a. Assonance
b. Rhyme
c. Line breaks
d. Alliteration

3. In dramatic texts (plays or scripts), which of the following are usually in italics to set them apart from other parts of the play?

a. Dialogues
b. Acts and scenes
c. Stage directions
d. Character tags

4. What structural feature is used to list items separately, making facts and ideas easier to see and understand?

a. Boldface
b. Bullet points
c. Sidebars
d. Headings

5. If an author writes about cats and dogs, showing their similarities and differences, this would be an example of what type of organizational pattern?

a. Cause and effect
b. Problem and solution
c. Proposition and support
d. Compare and contrast

6. What sound device appeals to the reader's sense of hearing by using words that copy the noises objects or people make (for example, pow or whoosh)?

a. Onomatopoeia
b. Alliteration
c. Assonance
d. Consonance

Chapter Quiz Answer Key

1. A: See section **Children's Literature**

2. D: See section **Alliteration, Assonance, and Consonance**

3. C: See section **Text Structure in Drama**

4. B: See section **Structural Features of Informational Text**

5. D: See section **Compare and Contrast**

6. A: See section **Onomatopoeia**

Author's Purpose and Craft

Author's Purpose

An author may write a text for many different purposes. Four of the most common purposes are to inform, to persuade or influence, to express, or to entertain readers.

Informational Texts

- Inform the reader on a topic that they previously knew nothing about, such as many non-fiction texts.
- For example, an informative paper on kangaroos would detail where kangaroos live, what they look like, what they eat, and other habits.
- Informational texts are usually non-fiction, such as articles or instructions. They usually follow structures such as order of importance, problem and solution, or compare and contrast.

Persuasive Texts

- Influence the reader to think a certain way about a topic, calling them to action or pointing them toward resources that would help them to learn more about the topic.
- For example, an author may try to persuade the reader that waterparks are the best place to go in the summer when it is hot outside. The author would present information about waterparks and explain *why* they are good places to visit.
- Persuasive texts can be either fiction or non-fiction. They usually follow a structure such as proposal and support or cause and effect.

Expressive Texts

- Express the author or speaker's opinion or emotions about a topic. Lots of descriptive words are used to clearly show the reader how the author or speaker feels.
- For example, the author may think that a new playground in town is a good idea, and write an essay about why a playground would be great for the community.

Entertaining Texts

- Entertain the reader, such as in most fictional texts.
- For example, Astrid Lindren, the author of *Pippi Longstocking*, entertains her readers with the story of a year in the life of a young girl named Pippilotta, who goes on wild adventures with her horse and a monkey named Mr. Nilsson.
- Entertaining texts can be either fiction or non-fiction, but are usually stories such as a fairy tale or fictional piece of writing. Entertaining texts usually follow a chronological order.

Authors usually write to entertain, to inform, or to persuade their readers. The organization structure or pattern they use is related to what the author's purpose is. It is important to choose the pattern that best presents the information, as not all patterns will work for every piece of writing.

Example

Read the following sentence. State the author's point in writing the sentence, whether it is to inform, persuade, express an opinion, or entertain:

> The rollercoaster reached a peak and paused for a second, before gliding down the other side of the hill with a roar.

The purpose of the sentence is to entertain the reader. The author does not state his or her opinion on the topic, and the sentence doesn't inform the reader about an important topic. The sentence does not persuade the reader to accept a certain point of view, and is instead meant to entertain the reader by giving them the feeling they might get from riding an exciting roller coaster.

Notice that the text describes an event, rather than an issue or conflict. The event is part of a larger tale, where a series of events occur to form an entire story. The reader may notice that the author uses descriptive words to present the setting, such as gliding and roar. The reader can better picture a story when the setting is clearly presented.

Example

Read the following sentence and state the author's point in writing the sentence, whether it is to inform, entertain, persuade, or state an opinion:

> The new student handbook makes it against the rules to wear roller skates inside the school buildings.

The purpose of this sentence is to inform the reader. The sentence does not state an opinion on the topic, nor is it meant to entertain the reader. The sentence also does not persuade the reader to accept a certain point of view. The sentence gives information to the reader that they need to know in order to avoid breaking the rules.

Example

Read the following sentence from *Esperanza Rising* by Pam Munoz Ryan and state the author's purpose in writing the sentence: whether it is to inform, entertain, persuade, or state an opinion:

> "Our Land is alive, Esperanza...This whole valley breathes and lives..." He picked up a handful of earth and studied it. "Did you know that when you lie down on the land, you can feel it breathe? That you can feel its heart beating."

The purpose of the sentence is to entertain the reader. The sentence does not tell the reader important information about a specific topic, it is simply used as part of a greater fictional story meant for entertainment, in this case, about a legend that the land is alive. The sentence does not persuade the reader to accept a certain point of view, nor does it state an opinion.

When an author wishes to persuade the reader to accept a certain point of view, evidence is used to back-up a claim. If the author wants to state an opinion, that opinion is included within the text. Sentences that are meant to inform contain facts that the reader needs to know and are not often found in fictional stories.

Print and Graphic Features

An author may show information in a chart, a graph, in paragraph format, or as a list. Information may also be shown in a picture or a diagram. The way an author chooses to show information is often based on the purpose of the text and the audience that the text is meant to reach.

A reader may be asked to answer questions based on the graphic by itself, how the graphic relates to the text, or how the text would best be shown in a graphic form. Some common examples of graphics are cause and effect organizers, circle graphs, bar graphs, illustrations, and diagrams.

Cause and Effect Graphic Organizers

Cause-and-effect graphic organizers are often used to map the **elements of a story**. A reader might read a story about a string of events and then be asked to correctly fill in either the **cause** or **effect** of an event in the story.

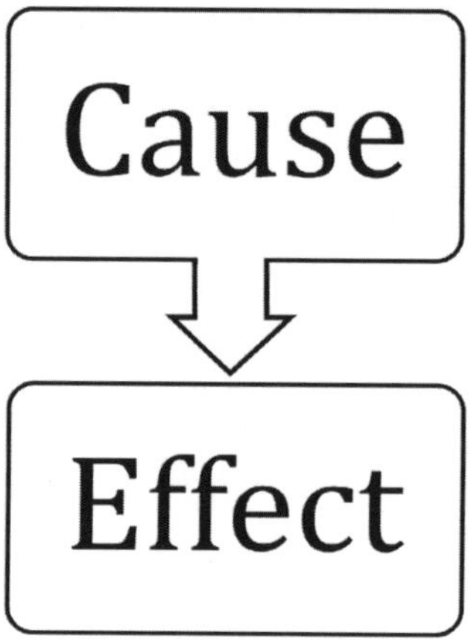

EXAMPLE

Read the following excerpt from *Ramona Quimby, Age 8* by Beverly Cleary and decide what the cause of the hectic morning at the Quimby house is.

> With all four members of the family leaving at different times in different directions, mornings were flurried in the Quimby household.

A **cause and effect** graphic organizer for this excerpt might look something like this:

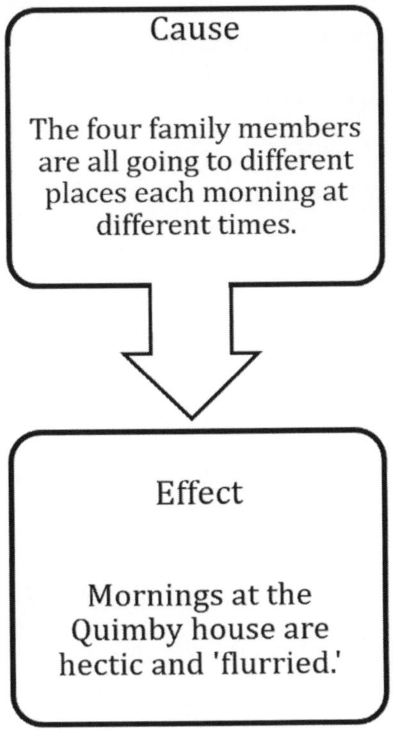

CIRCLE GRAPHS

Circle graphs, also called pie charts, are often used to represent information that can be shown as **parts of a whole**. For example, this graph shows the results of people being asked about their favorite color:

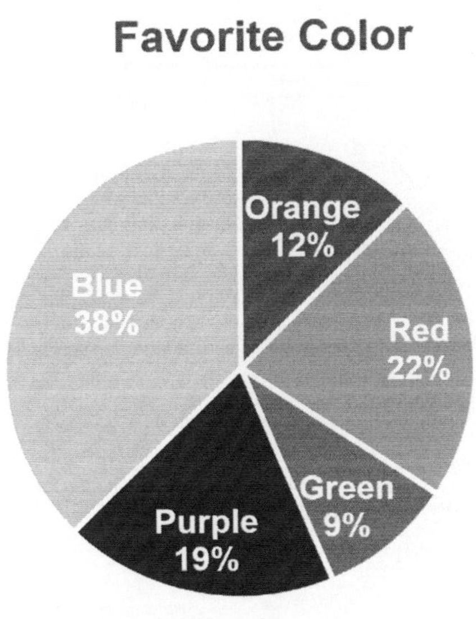

Bar Graphs

Bar graphs are used to show information about **numbers**. For example, this graph is a different way of representing the same results as those in the circle graph.

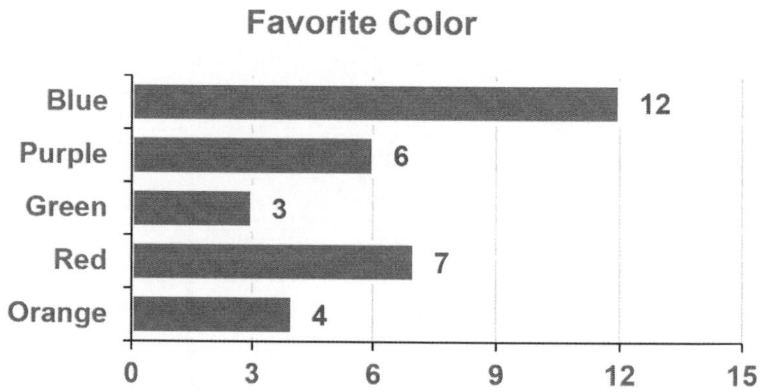

Illustrations and Photographs

Authors may choose to include **illustrations** or **photographs** (or both) with their texts. These two image types both show something from the text or give more information about the text.

Illustrations are drawings of an object. They may be based on reality, or they may represent an artist's abstract idea. For example, this is an illustration of a 1903 automobile:

Photographs are pictures of objects. They are generally extremely realistic, and most often show an object as it actually existed at that moment in time. For example, this is a photograph of a 1917 automobile:

Both illustrations and photographs give the reader another way to relate to and understand the text. The reader may be asked how the image relates to the text, what type of caption the image should be given, or why the author chose to include the image with the text.

DIAGRAMS

Diagrams are used to show information in a visual way. There are many different types of diagrams, including:

Diagrams that show the parts of an object, how they work together, or how they should be put together. This is an example of a diagram which shows how gears turn together

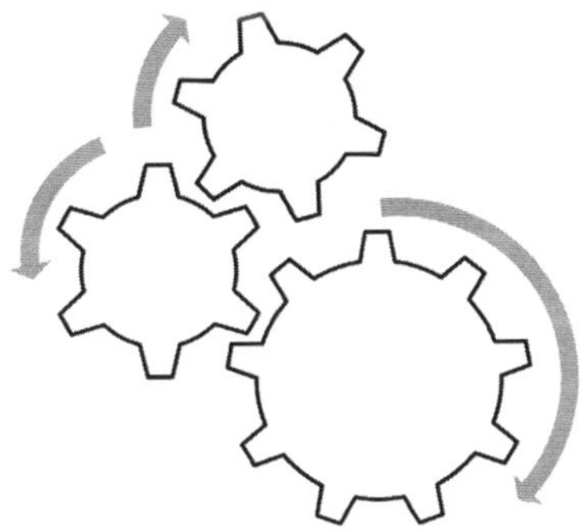

Diagrams that show how information is related are called **Venn Diagrams**. These are ways to visually see the way in which two different ideas overlap. This is an example of a Venn Diagram comparing cats and dogs:

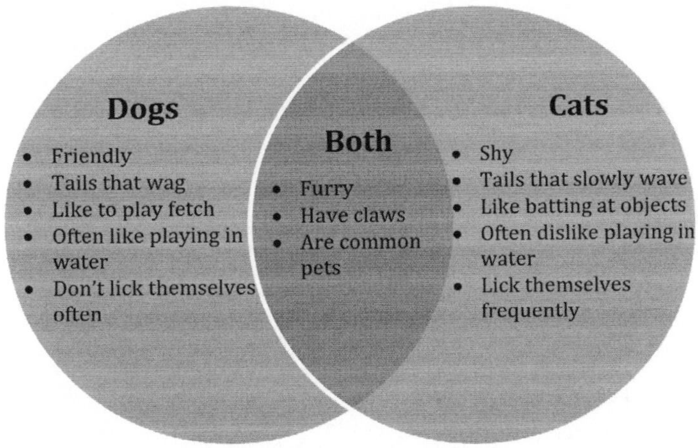

IMAGERY

Imagery is the use of **descriptive language** to add life or feeling to a work of literature. Many authors add literary and sound devices to create vivid pictures in the minds of their readers. Most of the time, imagery is thought to be one of the best ways to help readers fully understand and remember a work.

The most common forms of imagery are those that appeal to the sense of sight and sound. Imagery that appeals to the sense of sight, or **visual imagery**, helps the reader picture an event in their mind, usually by including specific details in the text that are not strictly necessary for the purpose of the story, but allow the reader to more easily "see" the scene. Some common forms of figurative language can help create visual imagery.

Review Video: Sensory Language Visit mometrix.com/academy and enter code: 177314

LITERAL AND FIGURATIVE LANGUAGE

Many types of text use both **literal language**, which means just what it says, and **figurative language**, which means something more than the literal words being used. Figurative language is a literary device that allows the author to expand reality in a vivid way. When an author uses figurative language, she connects things in an exaggerated way in order to create a memorable image, which helps to describe a situation in a new way for the reader.

Review Video: Figurative Language
Visit mometrix.com/academy and enter code: 584902

SIMILE

- Shows similarity between two ideas or objects, using the words "**like**" or "**as**"
- For example, an author might write "The princess is as beautiful as a rose" to compare the appearance of a woman to a beautiful flower.

METAPHOR

- Puts one idea in place of another to draw a parallel between the two ideas.
- For example, an author might write "Her room was a pigsty," to compare a person's bedroom to a dirty spot where pigs sleep.

SYMBOLISM

- Using one object to stand for something else.
- For example, an author may include a flag flying high throughout a story to show pride in the characters' country and to represent the idea of patriotism.

HYPERBOLE

- An extreme exaggeration of an idea.
- For example, a character might say "I'm starving to death!" to show that they are really hungry. Most of the time a character who says this is not literally going to die from hunger, they are just ready for a snack.

IRONY

- Uses sarcasm or humor (usually with an emphasis on the opposite) to show difference from literal meaning.
- For example, if a character says "Well today must be my lucky day!" after they left their homework on the kitchen table, they are being ironic. The irony used here helps show that it is definitely *not* the character's lucky day.

PERSONIFICATION

- Gives life or human characteristics to an inanimate object
- For example, if an author writes "The trees whispered to each other across the wide blue sky," they are using personification to help the reader imagine the scene. Trees are not human beings, so they do not whisper, but the image created in the reader stands out more than a literal description would.

EXAMPLE

Based on current knowledge, identify whether metaphor, simile, or hyperbole is used in this sentence:

The chiming bell was a beacon of hope for the downtrodden villagers.

A metaphor is used in this sentence to draw a parallel between "the chiming bell" and "a beacon of hope." The bell is being compared to something else in the sentence, which indicates the use of metaphor or simile, but the reader knows that the sentence does not contain a simile, because the words **like** and **as** are not used to show the comparison. The sentence also does not contain an exaggeration of facts, so the reader can see that hyperbole is not used.

POINT OF VIEW

Authors choose which character tells the story they are writing. This is called **point of view**. The point of view affects the story in many ways. There are three general types of point of view:

FIRST PERSON

- Tells a story through the eyes of one character.
- Uses the pronouns 'I,' 'me,' 'we,' and 'my.'
- The reader gets only one side of the story, without any other angles on what may have happened in the text

SECOND PERSON

- Tells a story using the pronoun 'you.'
- The least common point of view.

THIRD PERSON

- Tells a story about a character or group of characters from an outside viewpoint.
- Uses the words 'her', 'his,' 'they,' or a name to talk about a character or characters.
- A common way to show action in a story which allows the author to easily and realistically tell a story from more than one person's viewpoint.
- Gives readers a more complete view of a story as it is told from many different perspectives.
  - Gives readers a more complete view of a story as it is told from many different perspectives.

STEREOTYPES AND ANECDOTES

Sometimes authors will use devices that are based on their own or others' experiences to try to make a text more believable or relatable. An **anecdote** is a brief story authors may use to help the reader relate to the author or his or her purpose for writing. Anecdotes can illustrate the author's point a way that is more real, believable, and relatable to the reader. A **stereotype** is a generalization, or assumption, about a specific group of people. Authors can use stereotypes to help a reader understand that a character has a certain set of qualities and traits.

STYLE AND VOICE

Style and voice play an important role in the development of a story. The reader's impression of a story can vary based on the style and voice used by the author. **Style** refers to the way an author uses words, phrases, and sentence structure. The style of the text can change depending on whether the author uses short, choppy sentences, long, elaborate sentences, formal language, or informal language. **Voice** refers to the characteristics of a text that show the author's personality and distinguish the author from other writers. An author's voice may be recognized through the way they use words or the way they organize and present their thoughts. Voice is specific to each writer, and it can be as specific and unique as personality.

Chapter Quiz

1. An author's purpose in writing fiction is most often to:

a. Persuade
b. Inform
c. Entertain
d. Express

2. What is the least common point of view, that tells a story using the pronouns "you"?

a. First person
b. Second person
c. Third person
d. Narrator

3. What type of graphic can be used to visually see the way in which two different ideas overlap?

a. Circle graph
b. Bar graph
c. Venn diagram
d. Cause and effect organizer

4. What common form of figurative language puts one idea in place of another to draw a parallel between the two ideas?

a. Metaphor
b. Simile
c. Hyperbole
d. Irony

Chapter Quiz Answer Key

1. C: See section **Author's Purpose**

2. B: See section **Second Person**

3. C: See section **Diagrams**

4. A: See section **Metaphor**

Language

Vocabulary

DICTIONARY

A print or digital dictionary can be used to find out many things about a word. A dictionary will show the correct pronunciation of a word, provide its meaning, and identify what part of speech the word is. It will also tell how the word was derived—that is, what words it came from originally. A dictionary will have a **pronunciation guide** for each word that shows how to sound it out and where its syllables start and end. It will use symbols to indicate sounds, and will also use sample sounds (the "a" in "bad," for instance). A dictionary lists all of the meanings of a word and the parts of speech the word can be used as.

example \ ig-'zam-pəl\ noun

1. something that shows what a group of things is like
2. a model that should be either copied or avoided
3. a punishment meant to serve as a warning to others

EXAMPLE:

Julia used her dictionary to check the various meanings of the word *clear*. She found this entry:

clear (klîr) adjective

1. obvious.
2. easily seen through
3. free from flaw or blemish
4. free from guilt; untroubled
5. out of the way
6. to tidy *v*
7. to free *v*
8. to earn *v*

Identify which definition of *clear* is used in the following sentence:

Janet stood *clear* of the crowd pushing to get through the door.

The correct answer is meaning 5: "out of the way." If you substitute that definition for the word, the sentence makes sense. Meanings 1, 2, 3, and 4 do not fit with the context of the sentence. Meanings 6, 7, and 8 are verbs and "clear" as it is used in the sample is an adjective. When considering which meaning is being used, always check for context clues in the sentence or in the sentences before or after the sentence in which the word is used.

THESAURUS

A thesaurus is a reference book that gives **synonyms** of words. It is different from a dictionary because a thesaurus does not give definitions. A thesaurus can be helpful in finding the meaning of an unfamiliar word when reading. If the meaning of a synonym is known, then the meaning of the unfamiliar word will be known. Another time in which a thesaurus can be helpful is when writing. Using a thesaurus helps authors to vary their word choice.

GLOSSARY

A glossary is a **list of terms and their definitions** that can be found **at the back** of certain types of books, such as textbooks or reference books. A glossary does not have the definitions of all words, like a dictionary, but instead gives the definitions of the important terms within that particular book which are either uncommon or newly introduced. One may use a glossary when reading a book about economics or a chapter in a science textbook, for example, to define some of the technical terms within the text.

USING CONTEXT TO DETERMINE THE MEANINGS OF WORDS

Readers of all levels will encounter words that they have either never seen or that they have seen before but still don't know what it means. The best way to define a word in **context** is to look for nearby words that can assist in learning the meaning of the word.

CONTEXT CLUES

Context clues are hints about the meaning of a word. They are the words or phrases in the sentence or sentences before and after a new or unfamiliar word. Context clues give the reader an idea about what a word means. A context clue may also contain words that help define the new word or an example of what the new word means. Using context clues to figure out meaning can be helpful when learning a new set of vocabulary words or reading a difficult text. The dictionary definition of a word can always be looked up to double-check intended meaning.

SUBSTITUTION TO FIND MEANING

One way to find out if you have figured out the correct meaning of a new word is to **substitute** the meaning for the word. Using the example for *reluctant*, if the reader substituted in "not willing," the sentence would read

> Sam was "not willing" to be in the play, so he told the director that he was too busy to rehearse and didn't go to tryouts. He felt to shy to get up on a stage.

EXAMPLE

Using context clues, determine the meaning of the word *staggered* in the following sentence:

> As soon as he heard his Father's voice, he jumped up from his seat to open the door, but, as he did so, he *staggered* and fell headlong to the floor.

In the example, the word *staggered* refers to the action the character was taking before he "fell headlong to the floor". The reader knows that the character was on his feet, but that he did not have his balance. This information helps the reader decide that the word *staggered* means to move unsteadily.

Synonyms and Antonyms

When you understand how words relate to each other, you will discover more in a passage. This is explained by understanding **synonyms**, which are words that mean the same thing, and **antonyms**, which are words that mean the opposite of one another. As an example, *dry* and *arid* are synonyms, and *dry* and *wet* are antonyms.

Review Video: What are Synonyms and Antonyms?
Visit mometrix.com/academy and enter code: 105612

Example

Read the following sentences and determine the meaning of the word *reluctant* based on context clues:

> Sam was *reluctant* to be in the play, so he told the director that he was too busy to rehearse and didn't go to tryouts. He felt too shy to get up on a stage.

In this example sentence, the words "too busy" show that Sam made an excuse about why he couldn't be in the school play. The sentence also says that he "didn't go to tryouts." The second example sentence has other clues. It says, "He felt too shy to get up on stage." These clues give the reader hints about what the word *reluctant* means. It means "not willing."

Multiple-Meaning Words

A multiple-meaning word has different definitions, depending on the contextual use of the word. A multiple-meaning word is also called a **homonym**. A homonym is defined as a word that has more than one meaning, but is spelled and pronounced the same for all of them. For example, look at the word *leaves* in the following two sentences:

- Michelle *leaves* the building at 5 o'clock every day.
- The *leaves* fell off the oak tree in September.

In the first sentence, *leaves* means exits. In the second sentence, *leaves* refers to parts of a tree. By looking at the rest of each sentence, the reader can understand which definition of the multiple-meaning word the author is referring to.

Similar Words

Homophones are words that are pronounced the same, but may be spelled differently. An example of two homophones would be *heir* (someone due to inherit an estate) and *air* (the invisible substance people breathe).

Homographs are words that are spelled the same, but may be pronounced differently. An example of a homograph is the word *row*, which is pronounced one way when used to mean a horizontal grouping and is pronounced another way when used to mean an argument.

Root Words, Prefixes, and Suffixes

A **root word** is the base word, before an affix, in the form of a prefix, infix, or suffix, is added onto it. Many affixes in the English language come from Latin or Greek origins. A **prefix** is added onto the beginning of a root word, an **infix** is added into the middle, and a **suffix** is added onto the end of a root word. By looking at the meaning of a root word and the meaning of any affixes added to it, the reader can figure out the approximate meaning of the word. For example, the root word 'like' means to enjoy and the prefix 'dis-' means not. The reader can therefore understand that the full word 'dislike' means to not enjoy.

A reader can use root words and affixes to figure out the general meaning of an unknown word. Knowing root words and affixes is helpful on tests where analogies are made using unfamiliar words. By figuring out the general meaning of a new word, a tester can figure out the general relationship presented between two words.

Common Greek Root Words

Root	Meaning	Example
auto	self	automobile (a self-propelled vehicle)
geo	earth or ground	geography (study of the earth)
photo	light	photon (a small particle of light)

Common Prefixes

Prefix	Meaning	Example
trans-	across, through, or change	translate (to write or say in a different language)
super-	over or greater than	superhuman (greater than a regular human)
sub-	under	submerge (to sink below the surface)

Common Suffixes

Suffix	Meaning	Example
-ive	cause to, tend to, or doing	creative (a person who tends to make new things or think of new ideas)
-logy	study of	biology (study of life)
-ful	full of	wonderful (full of wonder)

Example

Using knowledge of affixes, determine meaning of the word *attentive* in the following sentence

> Jorge was a very *attentive* student in Social Studies class, but in Math, he often lost focus.

The word *attentive* contains the suffix "-ive," which means cause to, tend to, or doing. Readers may recognize the beginning of the word, "attent" as the same beginning as the word "attention." Based on the context, the reader can infer that this word means Jorge tends to pay attention in class, especially because of the contrast shown by the second half of the sentence.

Adages

Adages are sayings that describe something that is generally true. For example, "actions speak louder than words" is an **adage**. This adage means that a person's actions show their character more than their words do. Sometimes, adages use figurative language to communicate their true meanings. For example, the saying "the early bird gets the worm" is another adage. This saying means that those who take an opportunity as soon as they can, instead of waiting until later, will be rewarded. Even though the saying's meaning has nothing to do with birds or worms, the saying uses this image to help the recipient understand its real meaning.

Puns

A pun is a phrase that uses a word in an unusual way. **Puns** are usually used to entertain. An example of a pun is found in this excerpt from Lewis Carroll's *Alice's Adventures in Wonderland*:

> *'Mine is a long and a sad tale!' said the Mouse, turning to Alice, and sighing. 'It is a long tail, certainly,' said Alice, looking down with wonder at the Mouse's tail; 'but why do you call it sad?' And she kept on puzzling about it while the Mouse was speaking.*

The author creates a pun using the words "tail" and "tale." In the story, this confuses Alice, but it is meant to entertain the reader.

Chapter Quiz

1. A thesaurus can do all of the following, EXCEPT:

a. Give synonyms of words
b. Give word definitions
c. Help find the meaning of an unfamiliar word
d. Help authors vary their word choice when writing

2. Which of the following are words that sound alike, but are spelled differently and have different meanings?

a. Synonyms
b. Antonyms
c. Homophones
d. Homographs

3. Which of the following is a saying that describes something that is generally true?

a. Adage
b. Pun
c. Analogy
d. Idiom

Chapter Quiz Answer Key

1. B: See section **Thesaurus**

2. C: See section **Similar Words**

3. A: See section **Adages**

Spelling

Vowels and Consonants

Vowels and consonants describe the sounds in the English language. **Vowels** are the sounds made with only the voice, such as /a/, /e/, /i/, /o/, and /u/. Sometimes the letter y can make an /i/ sound. Consonants make up all of the other sounds in English. Consonants are sounded out by using the tongue, teeth, and lips.

Syllables

Syllables are the individual sounds that make up spoken words. Syllables can be determined by saying a word out loud and listening to what the individual sounds are. Some people split sounds up differently, but the important part of syllables is knowing where each sound in a word starts and stops.

One Syllable	Two Syllable	Three Syllable	Four Syllable
Bat	Draw-ing	Ba-tter-y	Com-for-ta-ble
Car	Foot-ball	Com-put-er	In-vis-i-ble
Home	Wa-ter	Flam-in-go	Wat-er-mel-on

Sometimes, words are diagrammed using the letters v and c to describe the vowels and consonants in the word. This helps to determine what types of syllables the word contains.

	Closed Syllables	Open Syllables	VCe Syllables
Word	Cat	Banana	Ripe
Pronunciation	/Kat/	/Buh-Na-Nuh/	/Rīp/
Syllables	CVC	CV-CV-CV	CVC

Notice how in the first example, cat is one syllable, which is made up of a consonant sound from the letter c, a vowel from the letter a, and another consonant sound from the letter t. In the second example, banana is three syllables, each of which has a consonant followed by a vowel.

Closed Syllables

Closed syllables are the easiest to recognize. They are marked by a consonant sound closing off the beginning or end of a syllable.

Open Syllables

Open syllable refers to the beginning or end of a syllable that does not have a consonant closing it off. Examples of this include the words *egg* and *blue.* The number and placement of consonants in different open syllables can affect the way the vowel is pronounced in each syllable.

	VCCV	VCV
Word	Tennis, Method	Robin, Tiger
Pronunciation	/Ten-is/, /Meth-od /	/Rob-in/, /Tī-ger/
Syllables	VC/CV, VCC/V	VC/V, V/CV

VCe Syllables

VCe syllables refer to words that have a silent e in them. The letter e is included to help identify the word when reading it, but the e sound is not spoken. Examples of words with silent e sounds are *bite*, *cake*, *flute*, and *tube*.

VV Syllables

When two vowels appear next to each other in a word, they may work together to make a single sound. However, when the vowels do not make one sound together, they mark the end of one syllable and the beginning of another syllable. These are VV syllables, also called vowel teams. For example, *duel*, *flour*, and *diary* all contain VV syllables.

R-Controlled Vowel Syllables

R-controlled syllables are formed when an *r* comes after a vowel. In r-controlled syllables, the vowel is paired with the *r* and makes a unique sound. Examples of words with r-controlled syllables are *jar*, *teacher*, *fir*, *torn*, and *spur*.

Final Stable Syllables

When a word ends in a Cle syllable, or a consonant followed by *le*, it has a final stable syllable. The syllable is made of these three letters. Examples of words with final stable syllables are *spectacle*, *thimble*, and *giggle*.

Affixes and Root Words

Affixes are syllables attached to the beginning or end of a word to adjust its meaning. Both prefixes and suffixes are affixes. A **prefix** is a syllable that appears at the beginning of a word that adjusts the root, or base, word' s meaning. For example, the prefix *mis* means wrong. When combined with the root word *spelling*, the word *misspelling* is created, which means wrong spelling. A **root word** is the base of a word that can have affixes added to it. For example, the suffix *-er* can be added to the root word *manage* to create *manager*, which means a person or thing who manages. The suffix -*able*, meaning capable of, can be added to *manage* to create *managable*, which means capable of being managed. Keep in mind that not every prefix and suffix can be simply added to a root word, since adding an affix will sometimes require some other spelling changes for the root word.

Common Prefixes

Prefix	Definition	Examples
anti-	against, opposing	antigravity, antidote
com-	with, together, very	community, combine
de-	from	depart, detangle
dis-	away, off, down, not	dislike, disappear
ex-	out	extract, exterior
inter-	among, between	intersection, interstate
mis-	bad, poorly, not	mistake, misspell, misunderstand
non-	not	nonexistent, nonsense
over-	above, in excess	overdone, overhead
post-	after, following	postpone, postscript
pre-	before, previous	prevent, premade
pro-	forward, in place of	propel, pronoun
retro-	back, backward	retrospect, retrograde
semi-	half, partly	semicircle, semicolon
sub-	under, beneath	submarine, subject
super-	above, extra	superstore, supervise
re-	backward, again	repeat, redo
trans-	across, beyond, over	transform, transport, transit
un-	not, reverse of	unhappy, unlock
uni-	one	uniform, unity

Common Suffixes

Suffix	Definition	Examples
-able or -ible	capable of being	suitable, edible
-ation	action, state, result	occupation, federation, starvation
-dom	state, rank, condition	kingdom, wisdom
-en	cause to be, become	deepen, strengthen
-er or -or	role, function	teacher, elevator
-ess	feminine	waitress, actress
-ful	filled with, marked by	thankful, hateful
-hood	state, condition	falsehood, statehood
-ion	action, result, state	union, confusion
-ish	suggesting, like	feverish, childish
-ist	worker, status, follower	dentist, finalist, colonist
-ity or -ty	state, quality, condition	ability, faulty
-ize	cause to be, treat as	realize, emphasize
-less	lacking, without	hopeless, countless
-ment	result, action	refreshment, employment
-ness	quality, state	greatness, dullness
-ous	marked by, given to	religious, gracious
-ship	status, relationship, trait	penmanship, friendship

Spelling Changes with Suffixes

When a suffix is added to the root word, usually the resulting word is spelled just like the root word and the suffix put together. However, there are some words that will require other spelling changes when a suffix is added. These changes include doubling consonants, removing *e*, and changing *y* to *i*.

Double Consonants

Most words that end in a closed syllable with one closing consonant will need the final consonant doubled if a suffix is being added.

Adding -ing: fibbing, submitting, running

Adding -er: sadder, flipper, hummer

Adding -est: biggest, flattest, hippest

Removing E

Many words ending with a VCe syllable will lose the silent *e* when a suffix is added. This only applies if the first letter of the suffix is a vowel.

Root Words Ending in Y

If the root word ends with a consonant and a *y*, when a suffix is added, an *i* will replace the *y*.

Adding -ness: silliness, readiness, stickiness

Adding -ous: glorious, studious, industrious

Adding -ed: applied, satisfied, spied

Pronunciation Changes with Suffixes

Suffixes may change the way that letters are pronounced when a word is read aloud. It is important to know how to spell these words when adding suffixes, especially if the spelling does not seem to match the pronunciation.

For example, consider the suffixes *-ian* and *-ion*. When a word ends in *c*, *s*, or *t* and one of these two suffixes is added to it, the word may be pronounced with a *sh* or *zh* sound. However, the word will still be spelled using the *c*, *s*, or *t*.

> Examples with -ian: electric + ian=electrician | Egypt + ian=Egyptian

> Examples with -ion: fuse + ion=fusion | intersect + ion=intersection

Common Spelling Mistakes

Vowels

There must be a vowel in every word. If a writer spells a word without a vowel, he or she has made a mistake and should correct it. Not every word needs a consonant, and there are even some words that are made of one vowel, like *a* or *I*. If a word has more than one syllable, there should also be at least one vowel in every syllable. However, there are words and syllables that do not contain *a*, *e*, *i*, *o*, and *u*. In these words and syllables, *y* acts as a vowel.

I Before E

If a word contains the letters *i* and *e* right next to each other, the *i* usually goes before the *e*, such as in *relieve*. However, if the two letters come right after a *c*, then the *e* should go before the *i*, such as in *receipt*. Also, if the two letters make a long *a* sound when spoken aloud, the *e* should go before the *i*, such as in *their*. Several words do not follow these rules, so it is best to double-check the spelling of confusing words in the dictionary.

Word Confusion

To, Too, and Two

To can be an adverb or a preposition for showing direction, purpose, and relationship. A dictionary can also be used to see the many other ways to use *to* in a sentence.

> Examples: I went to the store. | I want to go with you.

Too is an adverb that means *also, as well, very,* or *in excess.*

> Examples: I can walk a mile too. | You have eaten too much.

Two is a number.

> Example: You have two minutes left.

There, Their, and They're

There can be an adjective, adverb, or pronoun. Often, *there* is used to show a place or to start a sentence.

Examples: I went there yesterday. | There is something in his pocket.

Their is a pronoun that is used to show ownership.

Examples: He is their father. | This is their fourth apology this week.

They're is a contraction of *they are.*

Example: Did you know that they're in town?

Its and It's

Its is a possessive pronoun that shows ownership.

Example: The guitar is in its case.

It's is a contraction of *it is.*

Example: It's an honor and a privilege to meet you.

Affect and Effect

There are two main reasons that *affect* and *effect* are so often confused: 1) both words can be used as either a noun or a verb, and 2) unlike most homophones, their usage and meanings are closely related to each other. Here is a quick explanation of the four usage options:

Affect (n): feeling, emotion, or mood that is displayed

Example: The patient had a flat *affect.* (i.e., his face showed little or no emotion)

Affect (v): to alter, to change, to influence

Example: The sunshine *affects* the plant's growth.

Effect (n): a result, a consequence

Example: What *effect* will this weather have on our schedule?

Effect (v): to bring about, to cause to be

Example: These new rules will *effect* order in the office.

Chapter Quiz

1. Which of the following words has three syllables?

a. Invisible
b. Battery
c. Drawing
d. Football

2. When a word ends in a Cle syllable, or a consonant followed by *le* (for example, spectacle, thimble, or giggle), it has what type of syllable?

a. VCe syllable
b. VV syllable
c. Final stable syllable
d. R-controlled syllable

3. All of the following prefixes can mean "not" EXCEPT for:

a. dis-
b. ex-
c. non-
d. un-

4. When adding a suffix to most words that end in a closed syllable with one closing consonant (for example, sad or flip), what change needs to be made to the root word?

a. No change is needed
b. Add a y before the suffix
c. Add a silent e
d. Double the final consonant

5. If a word contains the letters *i* and *e* right next to each other, the *i* usually goes before the *e*, EXCEPT when the two letters come right after:

a. C
b. F
c. N
d. T

6. There, they're, and their are commonly misspelled homophones. Which one is a pronoun that is used to show ownership?

a. There
b. They're
c. Their
d. All of the above

Chapter Quiz Answer Key

1. B: See section **Syllables**

2. C: See section **Final Stable Syllables**

3. B: See section **Common Prefixes**

4. D: See section **Double Consonants**

5. A: See section **I Before E**

6. C: See section **There, Their, and They're**

Writing Process

Brainstorming

When choosing what to write about, activities like brainstorming can help inspire new ideas or help writers see how their ideas go together. **Brainstorming** means considering a variety of topics or ideas and is mainly used to find a creative approach to a subject or problem. A good first step in brainstorming is simple **free-association** with a topic. One way of doing this is sitting down with paper and pen and writing every thought that comes to mind about the topic in a word or phrase. It does not matter how helpful or good the thought seems at first; the writer should write down everything that comes to mind about the topic. Then, the writer should read the list over a few times. Next, he or she should look for patterns, repetitions, and clusters of ideas. This allows a variety of fresh ideas to come as the writer thinks about the topic.

Free Writing

Free writing is a more organized form of brainstorming. **Free writing** means taking a limited amount of time, like 2 to 3 minutes, to write everything that comes to mind about a topic in complete sentences. When the time is up, the writer should review everything he or she has written down. Many of the sentences may not make sense, but they may contain ideas and details that help the writer organize his or her ideas and prepare to plan the composition. Usually, free writing results in more useful ideas than brainstorming because the writer's thoughts and connections are written in complete sentences. However, both methods can be used together to help the writer prepare to plan and write a composition.

Mapping

Mapping an essay describes a couple of different methods. One method is using a graphic organizer with different tiers of ideas and details. The other method is similar to outlining. Outlining usually means using a bulleted list to plan the purpose or main idea for each paragraph in an essay. Under each paragraph bullet, any details, ideas, or sources that are essential to that paragraph will be listed. Most outlines also include a working thesis at the beginning of the outline. The main difference between using an outline and mapping an essay is that mapping does not necessarily mean organizing information by paragraph. The process of mapping an essay will generally include many steps to an outline, such as beginning with a thesis and using a bulleted list, but each point will not always represent one paragraph. This can be very helpful for essay planning because it allows writers to see how their ideas flow and allows them to consider the structure of the essay and make some changes before they begin writing.

Planning

Planning is the process of organizing a piece of writing before writing a draft. At the beginning of planning, writers should decide **why they are writing** and **who will read what they write**. The writer must also choose a **genre**, which is the **type** of composition he or she will write. There are fiction genres, such as comedy, folklore, action, and mystery. There are also nonfiction genres, such as essays, reports, poems, and journals. To plan his or her composition, a writer may create an outline or a graphic organizer, such as a Venn diagram, a spider-map, or a flowchart. These methods should help the writer choose their topic, main ideas, and how to organize the composition. If the writer needs to do research for the composition, he or she may also do so as they plan. Planning helps writers organize all of their ideas and decide if they have enough information to begin their first draft. However, writers should remember that the decisions they make during planning may change later, so their plan does not have to be perfect.

Drafting

Writers may then use their plan, outline, or graphic organizer to compose their first draft. They may write more drafts after the first one to improve their writing. Writing multiple drafts can help writers think of different ways to state their ideas and correct mistakes that may be hard to fix without rewriting a section of the composition, or the whole composition. There is no "right" number of drafts, so different writers may write a different number of drafts. Writing drafts also makes it easier to write freely because a writer can improve his or her composition with each draft they write.

Revising, Editing, and Proofreading

Once a writer completes a draft, he or she can move on to revising, editing, and proofreading to improve the draft. **Revising** is making sure that the composition is right for the audience, is not missing important information, is on topic, and is well organized. Revising may happen after the first draft so that errors are not repeated in the next draft. Each draft should be revised before the next one is written so that no mistakes are missed. **Editing** comes next. Editing a composition includes steps like improving transitions between paragraphs and making sure each paragraph is on topic. While editing, the writer must pay attention to the words he or she uses and the way the information in each paragraph is organized. Writers may also fix grammar mistakes in the editing phase, since some errors will require a writer to rewrite large parts of their work. **Proofreading** means fixing misspelled words, errors in grammar, and any other small mistakes in the composition.

During the revising, editing, and proofreading steps, it can be helpful for writers to ask a peer to read their work, since he or she may notice mistakes or problems the writer missed before. A writer may also choose to read his or her own work aloud, or listen to someone else read it. Hearing a composition aloud can help writers find mistakes or opportunities for improvement in their work more easily. This happens because when something is read aloud, the person reading the text must pay closer attention to the words on the page. When a writer or a peer reads the composition, they should point out any sentence that confuses them the first time they read it. Most of these sentences can be revised in a way that makes it easier to read and understand.

Adding and Removing Information

While both revising and editing may involve changing the words in a composition, they can also involve adding or taking away words. When a writer has completed a draft and reread it, he or she may notice that something, such as a transition, important details, or an explanatory sentence, is missing. Simply changing the words to make the passage sound better will not solve this problem, so the writer must **add** whatever words and information is needed to make the passage make sense and achieve the writer's purpose.

In other cases, a writer may have words, a sentence, or sometimes an entire paragraph that gives unnecessary information or explains the information in a way that is confusing. When this happens, the extra words and information weaken the composition and must be **removed**. Sometimes, this is difficult for writers to do because it may require them to remove writing they are proud of or a fact they find interesting. Despite this, revising and editing are steps meant to improve and strengthen a composition, so the writer should change, add, or remove parts of his or her writing in a way that makes it better and achieves his or her purpose.

Revising Sentences

Sentence variety is important to consider when writing an essay. A variety of sentence lengths and types can make an essay more engaging, and different types of sentences can sometimes help readers better understand information. For example, a sentence containing a list may make more sense when written with a simple sentence structure, since writing a compound sentence containing a list may give the reader too much information at once. On the other hand, information that is closely related and can be connected with a conjunction should be written in a compound sentence, rather than a simple sentence, since a compound sentence helps the reader see that the information goes together.

Using only simple sentences often makes writing boring and bothersome to read. Writing using only compound sentences makes it difficult for writers to explain information well and difficult for readers to understand, since every sentence will include a coordinating conjunction. To check an essay for sentence variety, it is helpful to look at whether the essay contains different sentence structures and lengths. It is also important to pay attention to the way each sentence starts and avoid beginning with the same words or phrases.

Revising Vocabulary

When writing informational or argumentative texts, it is important to use **precise vocabulary**, or **word choice**, to explain your main idea and supporting details. Generalized vocabulary will not help the audience fully understand the points that you are attempting to make because it will not accurately explain your main idea and supporting details. Precise vocabulary is important to use because it will accurately describe the ideas that are central to your text. When you research a subject, make sure to familiarize yourself with any vocabulary that is involved in its explanation. Use context clues, dictionaries, or, if necessary, a technical dictionary to decode any words that you are not familiar with. Precise vocabulary also impacts the effectiveness of narrative text. Carefully choosing vocabulary to describe sensory details, or imagery, helps writers paint the best possible picture of the events they are describing through their writing.

Chapter Quiz

1. Which of the following means taking a limited amount of time, like 2 to 3 minutes, to write everything that comes to mind about a topic in complete sentences?

a. Brainstorming
b. Drafting
c. Mapping
d. Free writing

2. What is often the first step after a writer completes a draft, and involves making sure that the composition is right for the audience, it is not missing important information, is on topic, and is well organized?

a. Adapting
b. Editing
c. Proofreading
d. Revising

3. When revising sentences in an essay, which of the following is NOT good advice?

a. Avoid beginning sentences with the same words or phrases
b. Include a variety of sentence lengths
c. Improve understanding by only using compound sentences
d. Keep sentences simple when they include lists

4. In what step of the writing process does the writer decide why they are writing, who will read what they write, and what genre they want to write?

a. Brainstorming
b. Drafting
c. Mapping
d. Planning

Chapter Quiz Answer Key

1. D: See section **Free Writing**

2. D: See section **Revising, Editing, and Proofreading**

3. C: See section **Revising Sentences**

4. D: See section **Planning**

Essay Structure and Organization

Controlling Ideas and Supporting Details

In the first paragraph of a composition, writers include a sentence that explains the **controlling idea.** This sentence is also known as the **thesis**. The rest of the paragraph shows the reader why the topic of the essay is interesting and includes details that support the controlling idea. One way to understand the relationship between the controlling idea and supporting information is to think about a table: the tabletop is the controlling idea, and each of the table's legs is a supporting detail or group of details. All of the legs work together to support the tabletop and create a table, just like the supporting details work together to support the controlling idea and create a composition.

Introduction

The introduction is used to capture the reader's attention and announce the essay's controlling idea. Normally, the introduction contains about 3-5 sentences. An introduction can begin with an interesting quote, a question, a strong opinion, or something else that will **interest** the reader's and prompt them to keep reading. If the composition has a prompt, the introduction should **restate** or **summarize** some part of the prompt so that the reader will have an idea of what information will be in the essay. Finally, your introduction should include the **controlling idea**, the primary thing the essay will tell the reader.

Review Video: Introduction
Visit mometrix.com/academy and enter code: 961328

Body

In an essay's introduction, the writer states the controlling idea and prepares the reader for the information in the rest of the composition. In the body of the composition, the writer **explains**, **demonstrates**, and **gives more information about** the **controlling idea**. This is done using supporting details and examples that are relevant to the controlling idea of the composition. For example, if the composition's controlling idea is a vacation the writer took, the body will include descriptions of where the writer went, what they experienced, and what they thought of the trip. If the composition's controlling idea is the writer's opinion, the body will include examples and facts that show why he or she has formed that opinion. If composition's controlling idea is a topic and the writer wants to instruct the reader, the body will contain facts, explanations, and examples that help teach the reader about the controlling idea. A writer will use supporting details to explain the controlling idea throughout the body.

The body should also contain multiple paragraphs, and the order the writer puts these paragraphs in is important. Each paragraph should include at least one supporting detail, but a paragraph may include more than one if two or more supporting details work together to support the controlling idea. If the controlling idea is to describe something that happened, the paragraphs should match the order in which the events occurred. If the controlling idea is to present an opinion or instruct the reader, the paragraphs should be ordered in the way that would make the most sense to the reader. The order of body paragraphs is important because it can impact how easy a composition is to read.

Review Video: Drafting Body Paragraphs
Visit mometrix.com/academy and enter code: 724590

Paragraphs

After the introduction of a passage, the body paragraphs will explain and elaborate upon the controlling idea. While each paragraph should relate to the controlling idea of the composition, each paragraph should focus on one point or supporting detail. Normally, a paragraph has a good topic sentence that summarizes the paragraph's main point. A topic sentence is a sentence that gives an introduction to the paragraph and its contents. Topic sentences should contain information that is more specific than what is in the introduction and may include a supporting detail, but they should not contain explanations or examples.

Supporting Details

The next sentences in the paragraph should support the topic sentence. These sentences can contain examples, explanations, or other specific information that supports the topic sentence, which supports the controlling idea of the composition. While a paragraph may be structured in any way, as long as it logically provides information that supports the controlling idea, it can be best to use a template or pattern to make sure that each paragraph is complete and well organized. For example, a good template to follow is topic sentence, evidence, explanation, conclusion. This means that after the topic sentence, the next sentence should provide evidence, such as a quote or example, that shows that the supporting detail is true or relevant. Next, the paragraph should include a sentence that explains how the evidence supports the paragraph's main point. If there are multiple examples or quotes, more than one sentence may be used for each section. Finally, there should be a sentence that concludes the paragraph. The concluding sentence may be similar to the topic sentence, but it should help the reader understand the paragraph and prepare them for the next one.

Choosing Supporting Details and Examples

When writing an informative or argumentative text, writers must choose supporting details carefully. Including details that are irrelevant, inaccurate, or vague does not strengthen the author's writing, while relevant, accurate, provable, and specific details do strengthen the author's writing. These details can make the writer's meaning clearer or give evidence that the author's points are true or logical. Such details may include examples or facts, such as statistics, statements from others who have authority on the subject, and common events or experiences. Choosing appropriate supporting details can also help the author show that they put effort into forming their ideas. This can also make the composition more intriguing and enjoyable to read, since the writer's own interest and insight will be apparent to the reader.

Length of a Paragraph

A paragraph must contain enough information to support its main point and the composition's controlling idea. A paragraph of two or three sentences will most likely not support the main point or controlling idea because it is not likely to contain enough information, explanation, or evidence. When a paragraph does not support the main point or controlling idea, it does not help the writer achieve their purpose or goal for writing the essay. A helpful, informative paragraph will often have somewhere from three to five sentences.

Starting a New Paragraph

For most forms of writing, you will need to use multiple paragraphs. This means that deciding when to start a new paragraph is very important. Reasons for starting a new paragraph include:

- To separate the introduction and conclusion from the body paragraphs
- To move from one supporting detail or point to another
- To indicate an important shift in time or place
- To show a comparison, contrast, or cause and effect relationship

Transitions

Transitions between sentences and paragraphs guide readers from idea to idea and show relationships between sentences and paragraphs. Writers should use transitions carefully and only when they are truly helpful. They should also be selected to fit the author's purpose. Transitions can show relationships such as time, comparison, an order of events, and cause and effect. Transitions are often used at the beginning of a phrase, sentence, or paragraph, since this helps prepare the reader for the next piece of information.

Types of Transitional Words

Time	Afterward, immediately, earlier, meanwhile, recently, lately, now, since, soon, when, then, until, before, etc.
Sequence	too, first, second, further, moreover, also, again, and, next, still, besides, finally
Comparison	similarly, in the same way, likewise, also, again, once more
Contrasting	but, although, despite, however, instead, nevertheless, on the one hand... on the other hand, regardless, yet, in contrast.
Cause and Effect	because, consequently, thus, therefore, then, to this end, since, so, as a result, if... then, accordingly
Examples	for example, for instance, such as, to illustrate, indeed, in fact, specifically
Place	near, far, here, there, to the left/right, next to, above, below, beyond, opposite, beside
Repetition, Summary, or Conclusion	as mentioned earlier, as noted, in other words, in short, on the whole, to summarize, therefore, as a result, to conclude, in conclusion
Addition	and, also, furthermore, moreover

Review Video: Transition Words
Visit mometrix.com/academy and enter code: 707563

Conclusion

The conclusion of a composition should summarize the controlling idea and show that it has been explained well. A good conclusion shows the reader why the author's controlling idea is meaningful and important and how the supporting details should help the reader understand the controlling idea. The conclusion should also give the reader something to think about that is related to the controlling idea. For example, in the conclusion, the author can invite readers to think about how they feel or what they think after reading the composition. Some things to avoid when writing conclusions include:

- Introducing a completely new idea
- Apologizing for one's opinions or writing
- Repeating the controlling idea word for word rather than summarizing them
- Using the conclusion to summarize every detail in the composition

Review Video: Drafting Conclusions
Visit mometrix.com/academy and enter code: 209408

Chapter Quiz

1. "Too," "and," "next," "still," "besides," and "finally" are all what type of transitional word?

a. Time
b. Sequence
c. Comparison
d. Contrasting

2. Which of the following should be avoided in an essay conclusion?

a. Reminding the reader of the central idea by repeating it word for word
b. Showing the reader why the author's central idea is meaningful and important
c. Showing that the central idea has been explained well
d. Giving the reader something to think about that is related to the central idea

3. A helpful, informative paragraph will often have how many sentences?

a. One to three sentences
b. Three to five sentences
c. Five to ten sentences
d. Ten to fifteen sentences

4. The body of an essay should do all of the following, EXCEPT:

a. Introduce the central idea
b. Demonstrate the central idea
c. Explain the central idea
d. Give information about the central idea

Chapter Quiz Answer Key

1. B: See section **Types of Transitional Words**

2. A: See section **Conclusion**

3. B: See section **Length of a Paragraph**

4. A: See section **Body**

Grammar

Subjects and Predicates

Subjects

Every sentence needs a subject and a predicate. The **subject** of a sentence names who or what the sentence is about. The subject may be directly stated in a sentence, or the subject may be implied. The **complete subject** includes the simple subject and any **modifiers**, such as adjectives, articles, prepositions, and adverbs, that go with it. To find the complete subject, ask *Who* or *What* before the verb to complete the question. The answer, including any modifiers, is the complete subject. To find the **simple subject**, remove all of the modifiers in the complete subject.

Examples:

simple subject

The small, red car is the one that he wants for Christmas.

complete subject

simple subject

The young artist is coming over for dinner.

complete subject

Review Video: Subjects in English
Visit mometrix.com/academy and enter code: 444771

An imperative sentence is a sentence that gives someone instructions or makes a request to someone. In **imperative** sentences, the verb's subject is understood, but is not actually present in the sentence. For example, this about the sentence *Drive to the store.* This sentence is a command, and the subject is *you.* If the subject were directly stated, the sentence would be *You, drive to the store.* Another fact to consider is that, normally, the subject comes before the verb. However, the subject comes after the verb in sentences that begin with *There are* or *There was.*

Direct:

John knows the way to the park.	Who knows the way to the park?	John
The cookies need ten more minutes.	What needs ten minutes?	The cookies
By five o'clock, Bill will need to leave.	Who needs to leave?	Bill
There are five letters on the table for him.	What is on the table?	Five letters
There were coffee and doughnuts in the house.	What was in the house?	Coffee and doughnuts

Implied:

Go to the post office for me.	Who is going to the post office?	You
Come and sit with me, please?	Who needs to come and sit?	You

Predicates

In a sentence, there is always a predicate and a subject. The subject tells what the sentence is about, and the **predicate** explains or describes the subject.

Think about the sentence *He sings*. In this sentence, we have a subject, *He*, and a predicate, *sings*. This is all that is needed for a sentence to be complete. Most sentences contain more information, but if this is all the information that is given in a sentence, then it is a complete sentence.

Now, let's look at another sentence: *John and Jane sing on Tuesday nights at the dance hall.*

subject predicate

John and Jane sing on Tuesday nights at the dance hall.

Subject-Verb Agreement

Verbs **agree** with their subjects in number. In other words, singular subjects need singular verbs. Plural subjects need plural verbs. **Singular** is for **one** person, place, or thing. **Plural** is for **more than one** person, place, or thing. Subjects and verbs must also share the same point of view, as in first, second, or third person.

Review Video: Subject-Verb Agreement
Visit mometrix.com/academy and enter code: 479190

Number Agreement Examples:

singular subject singular verb

Single Subject and Verb: Dan calls home.

Dan is one person. So, the singular verb *calls* is needed.

plural subject plural verb

Plural Subject and Verb: Dan and Bob call home.

More than one person needs the plural verb *call*.

Person Agreement Examples:

First Person: I *am* walking.

Second Person: You *are* walking.

Third Person: He *is* walking.

Complications with Subject-Verb Agreement

Words Between Subject and Verb

Words that come between the simple subject and the verb do not affect subject-verb agreement.

Examples:

singular subject — singular verb

The joy of my life returns home tonight.

The phrase *of my life* does not affect the verb *returns*.

singular subject — singular verb

The question that still remains unanswered is "Who are you?"

Don't let the phrase "*that still remains*..." confuse you. The subject *question* goes with the verb *is*.

Compound Subjects

A compound subject is formed when two or more nouns joined by *and*, *or*, or *nor* act together as the subject of the sentence.

Joined by And

When a compound subject is joined by *and*, it is treated as a plural subject and requires a plural verb.

Examples:

plural subject — plural verb

You and Jon are invited to come to my house.

plural subject — plural verb

The pencil and paper belong to me.

Joined by Or/Nor

For a compound subject joined by *or* or *nor*, the verb must agree in number with the part of the subject that is closest to the verb.

Examples:

subject — verb

Today or tomorrow is the day.

subject — verb

Stan or Phil wants to read the book.

subject — verb

Neither the pen nor the book is on the desk.

subject — verb

Either the blanket or pillows arrive this afternoon.

Indefinite Pronouns as Subject

An indefinite pronoun is a pronoun that does not refer to a specific noun. Different indefinite pronouns are used as a singular noun, a plural noun, or change depending on how they are used.

Always Singular

Pronouns such as *each*, *either*, *everybody*, *anybody*, *somebody*, and *nobody* are always singular. This is because these pronouns always stand in for one person, place, or thing.

Examples:

singular subject — singular verb
Each of the runners has a different bib number.

singular verb — singular subject
Is either of you ready for the game?

Note: The words *each* and *either* can also be used as adjectives. For example, *each* person is unique. When one of these adjectives modifies the subject of a sentence, it is always a singular subject.

singular subject — singular verb
Everybody grows a day older every day.

singular subject — singular verb
Anybody is welcome to bring a tent.

Always Plural

Pronouns such as *both*, *several*, and *many* are always plural. This is because these pronouns always stand in for more than one person, place, thing, or idea.

Examples:

plural subject — plural verb
Both of the siblings were too tired to argue.

plural subject — plural verb
Many have tried, but none have succeeded.

Depend on Context

Pronouns such as *some*, *any*, *all*, *none*, *more*, and *most* can be either singular or plural depending on what they are representing in the context of the sentence.

Examples:

singular subject — singular verb
All of my dog's food was still there in his bowl.

plural subject — plural verb
By the end of the night, all of my guests were already excited about coming to my next party.

Other Cases Involving Plural or Irregular Form

Some nouns are **singular in meaning but plural in form**: news, mathematics, physics, and economics.

The *news is* coming on now.

Mathematics is my favorite class.

Some nouns are plural in form and meaning, and have **no singular equivalent**: scissors and pants.

Do these *pants come* with a shirt?

The *scissors are* for my project.

Note: Look to your **dictionary** for help when you aren't sure whether a noun with a plural form has a singular or plural meaning.

Example

Which word should go in the blank?

Joan and Susan ____ going to the store this evening.

a. Is
b. Are
c. Am
d. Was

Try using each choice in the sentence. Choice A, *is*, forms this sentence: Joan and Susan is going to the store this evening. There are two people, Joan and Susan, who are going to the store. This makes the subject of the sentence plural. *Is* is a singular verb, meaning it does not agree with the subject and cannot be the answer.

Choice B, *are*, forms this sentence: Joan and Susan are going to the store this evening. The subject of the sentence is still plural. But *are* is a plural verb! The subject and verb agree, so *are* is the correct answer.

Choice C, *am*, forms this sentence: Joan and Susan am going to the store this evening. *Am* is a singular verb, and it is also only used in first person, when the writer or speaker is referring to themself. The subject is plural, and the sentence is in third person, so *am* is not the correct answer.

Choice D, *was*, forms this sentence: Joan and Susan was going to the store this evening. *Was* is a singular verb, so it does not agree with the plural subject in this sentence.

COMPLEMENTS

A complement is a noun, pronoun, or adjective that is used to give more information about the subject or verb in the sentence.

DIRECT OBJECTS

A direct object is a noun or pronoun that takes or receives the **action** of a verb. A complete sentence does not need a direct object, so not all sentences will have them. When you are looking for a direct object, find the verb and ask *who* or *what*.

Examples:

> I took *the blanket.*
>
> Jane read *books.*

INDIRECT OBJECTS

An indirect object is a word or group of words that show how an action had an **influence** on someone or something. If there is an indirect object in a sentence, then you always have a direct object in the sentence. When you are looking for the indirect object, find the verb and ask *to*, *for*, *whom*, or *what*.

Examples:

> We taught [the old dog]ₐ [a new trick]ᵦ.

We taught the old dog (indirect object) a new trick (direct object).

I gave them (indirect object) a math lesson (direct object).

Review Video: Direct and Indirect Objects
Visit mometrix.com/academy and enter code: 817385

PHRASES

A phrase is a group of words that functions as a single part of speech, usually a noun, adjective, or adverb. A **phrase** is not a complete thought, and does not contain a subject, but it adds detail or explanation to a sentence, or renames something within the sentence.

CLAUSES

A clause is a group of words that contains both a subject and a predicate (verb). There are two types of clauses: independent and dependent. An **independent clause** contains a complete thought, while a **dependent (or subordinate) clause** does not. A dependent clause includes a subject and a verb, and may also contain additional information, but it cannot stand as a complete thought without being joined to an independent clause. Dependent clauses function within sentences as adjectives, adverbs, or nouns.

Example:

I am running (independent clause) because I want to stay in shape (dependent clause).

The clause *I am running* is an independent clause: it has a subject and a verb, and it gives a complete thought. The clause *because I want to stay in shape* is a dependent clause: it has a subject and a verb, but it does not express a complete thought. This is due to the fact that it begins with *because*, which shows that there is more information needed to complete the thought. This dependent clause adds detail to the independent clause to which it is attached.

Review Video: Independent and Dependent Clauses
Visit mometrix.com/academy and enter code: 556903

SENTENCE STRUCTURE

Sentence structure is based on the type and number of clauses in the sentence. Two common sentence structures are simple sentences and compound sentences:

SIMPLE

A simple sentence has one independent clause with no dependent clauses. A simple sentence may have a **compound subject** or a **compound verb**, or both.

Examples:

single subject: Judy; single verb: watered
Judy watered the lawn.

compound subject: Judy and Alan; single verb: watered
Judy and Alan watered the lawn.

single subject: Judy; compound verb: watered, pulled
Judy watered the lawn and pulled weeds.

compound subject: Judy and Alan; compound verb: watered, pulled
Judy and Alan watered the lawn and pulled weeds.

COMPOUND

A compound sentence has two or more independent clauses with no dependent clauses. Usually, the independent clauses are joined with a comma and a coordinating conjunction or with a semicolon.

Examples:

independent clause: The time has come; independent clause: we are ready
The time has come, and we are ready.

independent clause: I woke up at dawn; independent clause: the sun was just coming up
I woke up at dawn; the sun was just coming up.

Complex

A complex sentence has one independent clause and at least one dependent clause.

Examples:

Although he had the flu, (dependent clause) Harry went to work. (independent clause)

Marcia got married (independent clause) after she finished college. (dependent clause)

Review Video: Sentence Structure
Visit mometrix.com/academy and enter code: 700478

Sentence Fragments

Recall that a group of words must contain at least one **independent clause** in order to be considered a sentence. If it doesn't contain even one independent clause, it is called a **sentence fragment**.

Choosing the best steps for **repairing** a sentence fragment depends on what type of fragment it is. If the fragment is a dependent clause, it can sometimes be fixed by simply removing a subordinating word, such as *when*, *because*, or *if*, from the beginning of the fragment. Alternatively, a dependent clause can be joined to a closely related neighboring sentence. If the fragment is missing some required part, like a subject or a verb, it may be fixed by simply adding the missing part.

Examples:

Fragment: Because he wanted to sail the Mediterranean.

Removed subordinating word: He wanted to sail the Mediterranean.

Combined with another sentence: Because he wanted to sail the Mediterranean, he booked a Greek island cruise.

Example

Which of the following changes will NOT correct this sentence fragment?

Although she had found the coin first.

a. Remove *Although*.
b. Add a comma and *she let her brother keep it* after *first*.
c. Add *She let her brother keep the coin* before *although*.
d. Remove *first*.

Choice A suggests removing the word *although* to form the following sentence: She found the coin first. This option removes the subordinating conjunction to make the clause independent. The resulting sentence is complete, so removing *although* is an acceptable way to correct the fragment. Choice A is incorrect.

Choice B forms the following sentence: Although she had found the coin first, she let her brother keep it. A comma and an independent clause have been added to the sentence fragment to form a complex sentence. The resulting sentence is complete and written correctly, so choice B is incorrect.

Choice C forms the following sentence: She let her brother keep the coin although she had found the coin first. An independent clause has been added before the sentence fragment to form a complex sentence. This sentence is correctly written and complete, so choice C is an acceptable way to correct the fragment. Choice C is incorrect.

Choice D removes the word *first*, leaving *Although she had found the coin*. This is still a sentence fragment, since it is a single dependent clause. Choice D does not correct the fragment, so D is correct.

RUN-ON SENTENCES

Run-on sentences consist of multiple independent clauses that have not been joined together properly. Run-on sentences can be corrected in several different ways:

Join clauses properly: This can be done with a comma and coordinating conjunction, with a semicolon, or with a colon or dash if the second clause is explaining something in the first clause.

Example:

> **Incorrect**: I went on the trip, we visited lots of castles.
>
> **Corrected**: I went on the trip, and we visited lots of castles.

Split into separate sentences: This correction is best to use when the independent clauses are very long or when they are not closely related.

Example:

> **Incorrect**: The drive to New York takes ten hours, my uncle lives in Boston.
>
> **Corrected**: The drive to New York takes ten hours. My uncle lives in Boston.

Make one clause dependent: This is the easiest way to make the sentence correct and more interesting at the same time. It's often as simple as adding a subordinating word between the two clauses or before the first clause.

Example:

> **Incorrect**: I finally made it to the store and I bought some eggs.
>
> **Corrected**: When I finally made it to the store, I bought some eggs.

Reduce to one clause with a compound verb: If both clauses have the same subject, remove the subject from the second clause, and you now have just one clause with a compound verb.

Example:

> **Incorrect**: The drive to New York takes ten hours, it makes me very tired.
>
> **Corrected**: The drive to New York takes ten hours and makes me very tired.

Note: While these are the simplest ways to correct a run-on sentence, often the best way is to completely reorganize the thoughts in the sentence and rewrite it.

COMMA SPLICES

A comma splice is a specific error that may appear in a run-on sentence. When a sentence has two independent clauses, but the clauses are joined with only a comma, a **comma splice** is formed. Remember that if two independent clauses are joined with a comma, a coordinating conjunction is also needed. Most of the solutions for fixing run-on sentences can also be used to correct a comma splice.

EXAMPLE

Rick wants to go see a movie tomorrow he would miss his sister's recital.

Identify the change that would NOT correct this run-on sentence.

a. Add a comma after *tomorrow.*
b. Split it into two sentences between *tomorrow* and *he.*
c. Add a comma and but after *tomorrow.*
d. Add a subordinating conjunction to make one of the clauses dependent.

Choice A says to add a comma after *tomorrow*. This forms the following sentence: Rick wants to go see a movie tomorrow, he would miss his sister's recital. A comma has been used to join two independent clauses, but there is no coordinating conjunction. This choice forms a comma splice, so it is not an acceptable correction for this sentence. Choice A is the correct answer.

Choice B says to split the sentence into two sentences. This forms the following two sentences: Rick wants to go see a movie tomorrow. He would miss his sister's recital. Both of these sentences are complete. This is an acceptable way to correct the run-on sentence, so choice B is incorrect.

Choice C says to add a coordinating conjunction after *tomorrow*. This forms the following sentence: Rick wants to go see a movie tomorrow, but he would miss his sister's recital. A comma and a coordinating conjunction have been added between the two independent clauses. This is an acceptable way to correct a run-on sentence. Choice C is incorrect.

Choice D says to add a subordinating conjunction to make one of the sentences dependent. There are many new sentences that could be created by adding a subordinating conjunction. For example, consider the following sentence: Although Rick wants to go see a movie tomorrow, he would miss his sister's recital. Alternatively, the following sentence could also be created: Rick wants to go see a movie tomorrow even though he would miss his sister's recital. Both of these sentences have an independent clause and a dependent clause. These sentences are both complete and written correctly, so choice D is incorrect.

EXAMPLE

Identify the sentence that has a comma splice.

a. Tom stopped at the store to buy supplies and his family met him at the campsite.
b. The ball rolled into the living room quietly, but it still startled the dog.
c. Theresa brought her mom some flowers, her mom did not have a vase.
d. Sweet potatoes, pecans, and brown sugar are all ingredients in my cousin's sweet potato casserole.

Choice A has two independent clauses joined by a coordinating conjunction. This is incorrect because there should be a comma before the coordinating conjunction. While the sentence is written incorrectly, there is no comma, so this sentence does not have a comma splice. Choice A is incorrect.

Choice B has two independent clauses joined by a comma and a coordinating conjunction. This is the correct way to write a compound sentence, so there is no error here. Choice B is incorrect.

Choice C has two independent clauses joined by a comma. This is incorrect because independent clauses should be joined together by a comma and a coordinating conjunction. When the comma is present without a coordinating conjunction between two independent clauses, a comma splice is formed. This means that choice C is correct.

Choice D is a simple sentence that contains one independent clause. The only commas used in this sentence are used to separate items in a list. There are no clauses that need to be joined or errors related to commas, so choice D does not contain a comma splice. Choice D is incorrect.

Parts of Speech

Nouns

When you talk about a person, place, thing, or idea, you are talking about a **noun**. The two main types of nouns are **common** and **proper** nouns.

Common Nouns

Common nouns are generic names for people, places, and things. Common nouns are not usually capitalized.

Examples of common nouns:

People: boy, girl, worker, manager

Places: school, bank, library, home

Things: dog, cat, truck, car

Proper Nouns

Proper nouns name specific people, places, or things. All proper nouns are capitalized.

Examples of proper nouns:

People: Abraham Lincoln, George Washington, Martin Luther King, Jr.

Places: Los Angeles, California; New York; Asia

Things: Statue of Liberty, Earth, Lincoln Memorial

Note: When referring to the planet that we live on, capitalize *Earth*. When referring to the dirt, rocks, or land, lowercase *earth*.

Singular and Plural Nouns

Singular nouns name **one** person, place, thing, or idea. **Plural nouns** name **more than one** person, place, thing, or idea. Most nouns have both a singular and plural form. Many plural nouns are spelled like the singular noun with an *-s* at the end, but this is not true for all plural nouns. Singular nouns that already end in an *s*, *o*, *ch*, *sh*, or *x* usually end in *-es* when they are in the plural form. Singular nouns that end in a consonant followed by the letter *y* will usually lose the *y* and end in *-ies* in the plural form, and words that end with the letter *f* or *fe* will usually lose the *f* and end in *-ves*.

Some plural nouns have much different spellings than their singular form, and some plural nouns are spelled the same as their singular form. There are more rules for spelling plural nouns, but these are the most common spelling changes.

Examples of singular nouns:

Typical nouns: dog, pencil, girl, store, hope, stingray

Nouns ending in *s*, *o*, *ch*, *sh*, or *x*: mass, hero, lunch, polish, fox

Nouns ending in a consonant and *y*: puppy, baby, fairy, sky

Nouns ending in *f* or *fe*: self, life, calf, hoof

Examples of plural nouns:

Typical nouns: dogs, pencils, girls, stores, hopes, stingrays

Nouns ending in *s*, *o*, *ch*, *sh*, or *x*: masses, heroes, lunches, polishes, foxes

Nouns ending in a consonant and *y*: puppies, babies, fairies, skies

Nouns ending in a vowel and *f* or *fe*: selves, lives, calves, hooves

COLLECTIVE NOUNS

Collective nouns are the names for a group of people, places, or things that function like singular nouns. The following are examples of collective nouns: *class, company, dozen, group, herd, team,* and *public.* Collective nouns usually require an article, such as *a*, *an*, and *the*, which shows that the noun is a single unit. For example, a choir is a group of singers. Even though there are many singers in a choir, the word choir describes a single group. If we refer to the members of the group, and not the group itself, it is no longer a collective noun.

Incorrect: The *choir are* going to compete nationally this year.

Correct: The *choir is* going to compete nationally this year.

Incorrect: The *members* of the choir *is* competing nationally this year.

Correct: The *members* of the choir *are* competing nationally this year.

EXAMPLE

Find the error in the following sentence.

John, Mary, and Claudia are all on the finance committee, which decide how the school's money is spent.

a. After *Claudia*, *are* should be changed to *is.*
b. After *money*, *is* should be changed to *are.*
c. After *which*, *decide* should be changed to *decides.*
d. The sentence is written correctly.

Choice A says that *are* should be changed to *is*. In this sentence, *are* is the verb that goes with the compound subject, John, Mary, and Claudia. Since the subject is plural, the verb that goes with it must also be plural. *Is* is a singular verb, so this would not be an appropriate change to make. Choice A is incorrect.

Choice B says that *is* should be changed to *are*. In the original sentence, the verb *is* refers to the noun *money*. Even though *money* may refer to more than one unit of currency, it is a collective noun, so it acts as a singular noun. *Are* is a plural verb, so it should not accompany the singular noun *money*. Choice B is incorrect.

Choice C says *decide* should be changed to *decides*. In the present tense, *decide* is used with plural nouns. *Decide* refers to *committee* in this sentence. A committee is a group of multiple people, but it functions as a singular noun because it is a collective noun. This means that *decide* should not go with *committee* and should be replaced with *decides*. Choice C is correct!

Choice D says that this sentence has no errors. In this sentence, the verb *decide* is used to refer to the collective noun *committee*. Since *decide* functions like a plural verb in this sentence, it cannot go with a collective noun. This is an error in the sentence, so choice D is incorrect.

Pronouns

Pronouns are words that are used to stand in for nouns. There are several different types of pronouns, but the two main types are subjective and objective pronouns. **Subjective** nouns and pronouns that those that are the subject of a sentence. **Objective** nouns and pronouns are those that are an object in a sentence. Another important type of pronoun is the personal pronoun, which refers to people. Personal pronouns can be subjective or objective. **Possessive** nouns and pronouns show possession or ownership. Pronouns can also be singular or plural.

Singular

Subjective	Objective	Possessive
I	Me	My, Mine
You	You	Your, Yours
He	Him	His
She	Her	Her, hers
It	It	Its
Who	Whom	Whose

Plural

Subjective	Objective	Possessive
we	us	our, ours
you	you	your, yours
they	them	their, theirs

Reflexive: Reflexive pronouns are pronouns that function as the object of a sentence and refer to the subject. Examples of reflexive pronouns include *myself, yourself, himself, herself, itself, ourselves, yourselves*, and *themselves.*

Indefinite: Indefinite pronouns are used to refer to multiple nouns or an undefined noun. Examples of indefinite nouns include *all, any, each, everyone, either/neither, one, some*, and *several*.

Review Video: Nouns and Pronouns
Visit mometrix.com/academy and enter code: 312073

EXAMPLE

Everyone felt better about themselves after his encouraging speech.

Which type of pronoun is NOT used in the sentence above?

a. Personal
b. Reflexive
c. Indefinite
d. Possessive

Choice A says that there is a personal pronoun in this sentence. Remember that personal pronouns are pronouns that replace a specific person's name or a group of people's names in a sentence. Also, they are either subjective or objective pronouns. In this sentence, *everyone* is the subject that acts on the object *themselves*. Neither of these pronouns take the place of a specific person's name, so there are no personal pronouns in the sentence. Choice A is correct!

Choice B says that there are no reflexive pronouns in this sentence. Remember that a reflexive pronoun is one that mentions the subject as the object of the sentence. In this sentence, the subject is *everyone* and the object is *themselves. Themselves* is used to refer to *everyone*, so *themselves* functions as a reflexive pronoun. Choice B is incorrect.

Choice C says that there are no indefinite pronouns in this sentence. Indefinite pronouns are used to represent a person, group, or thing that is not specified. In this sentence, the pronoun *everyone* is used. *Everyone* refers to a group of people, but does not specify which people. *Everyone* is an indefinite pronoun, so choice C is incorrect.

Choice D says that there are no possessive pronouns in this sentence. Remember that possessive pronouns are used to replace the name of a person or an object that possesses something. In this sentence, the encouraging speech is *his* speech. The speech belongs to *him*, so *his* is a possessive pronoun. Choice D is incorrect.

VERBS

If you want to write a sentence, then you need a verb. Without a verb, you have no sentence. The verb of a sentence indicates action or being. In other words, the verb shows something's action or state of being or the action that has been done to something.

ACTION VERBS AND LINKING VERBS

Action verbs show what the subject is doing. In other words, an action verb shows action. **Linking verbs** link the subject of a sentence to a noun or pronoun. They can also link a subject to an adjective, so the linking verb helps create a description. You always need a verb if you want a complete sentence. However, linking verbs on their own cannot be a complete sentence. Any verb that shows a condition and connects to a noun, pronoun, or adjective that describes the subject of a sentence is a linking verb.

Action: He sings. | Run! | Go! | I talk with him every day. | She reads.

Linking:

Incorrect: I am.

Correct: I am John. | The roses smell lovely. | I feel tired.

Review Video: Action Verbs and Linking Verbs
Visit mometrix.com/academy and enter code: 743142

Verb Tenses

A verb **tense** shows the different form of a verb to point to the time of an action. The present and past tense are indicated by the verb's form. An action in the present, *I talk,* can change form for the past: *I talked*. However, for future tense, an auxiliary, or helping, verb is sometimes needed to show the change in form.

Present: I talk
Past: I talked
Future: I will talk

Present: The action happens at the current time.

Example: He *walks* to the store every morning.

Past: The action happened in the past.

Example: He *walked* to the store an hour ago.

Future: The action is going to happen later.

Example: I *will walk* to the store tomorrow.

Irregular Verbs

While most verbs gain the suffix -ed when used in the past tense, irregular verbs receive different spelling changes when they are written in the past tense. For example, *walk* is a regular verb, and it becomes *walked* when written in the past tense. However, *run* is an irregular verb because it becomes *ran* when written in the past tense.

Example

Which of the following words is a regular verb?

a. Run
b. Warn
c. Hold
d. Catch

Remember that regular verbs are verbs that end in *-ed* when they are written in the past tense. Irregular verbs are spelled differently in past tense.

Choice A says that *run* is a regular verb. What is the past tense of *run*? Is it *runned* or *ran*? The past tense of *run* is *ran*, so it is an irregular verb. Choice A is incorrect.

Choice B says that *warn* is a regular verb. The past tense of *warn* is *warned*, which means that *warned* is a regular verb Choice B is correct.

Choice C says that *hold* is a regular verb. What is the past tense of *hold*? Is it *holded* or *held*? The past tense of *hold* is *held*, so it is an irregular verb. Choice C is incorrect.

Choice D says that *catch* is a regular verb. What is the past tense of *catch*? Is it *catched* or *caught*? The past tense of *catch* is *caught*, so it is an irregular verb. Choice D is incorrect.

Adjectives

An **adjective** is a word that is used to modify a noun or pronoun. An adjective answers a question: *Which one? What kind?* or *How many?* Usually, adjectives come before the words that they modify, but they may also come after a linking verb.

> Which one? The *third* suit is my favorite.
>
> What kind? This suit is *navy blue*.
>
> How many? I am going to buy *four* pairs of socks to match the suit.

Review Video: Descriptive Text
Visit mometrix.com/academy and enter code: 174903

Comparison with Adjectives

Some adjectives are relative, and other adjectives are absolute. Adjectives that are **relative** can show the comparison between things. **Absolute** adjectives can also show comparison, but they do so in a different way. Let's say that you are reading two books. You think that one book is perfect, and the other book is not exactly perfect. It is not possible for one book to be more perfect than the other. Either you think that the book is perfect, or you think that the book is imperfect. In this case, perfect and imperfect are absolute adjectives.

Relative adjectives will show the different **degrees** of something or someone to something else or someone else. The three degrees of adjectives include positive, comparative, and superlative.

The **positive** degree is the normal form of an adjective.

> Example: This work is *difficult*. | She is *smart*.

The **comparative** degree compares one person or thing to another person or thing.

> Example: This work is *more difficult* than your work. | She is *smarter* than me.

The **superlative** degree compares more than two people or things.

> Example: This is the *most difficult* work of my life. | She is the *smartest* lady in school.

Review Video: Adjectives
Visit mometrix.com/academy and enter code: 470154

EXAMPLE

What type of adjective is used in the following sentence?

The day John got married was the happiest day of his life.

a. Absolute
b. Comparative
c. Positive
d. Superlative

First find the adjective. The noun that is being described is *day*, so the adjective is *happiest.* Remember the difference between the different types of adjectives. Can one day be happier than another? How many days are being compared?

Choice A says *happiest* is an absolute adjective. Absolute adjectives cannot have different degrees. This sentence says that it was the happiest day of John's life, which means that it was happier than other days in his life. This means that *happiest* cannot be an absolute adjective, so A is incorrect.

Choice B says *happiest* is a comparative adjective. Comparative adjectives are used to compare two nouns. If John's wedding day is the happiest day of his life, then that day is being compared to thousands of other days. Also, *happiest* has the suffix *-est*, which is used in superlative adjectives that compare more than two nouns. These two facts show that *happiest* is not a comparative noun, so B is incorrect.

Choice C says that *happiest* is a positive adjective. Positive adjectives are the types of adjectives that simply describe nouns, but can be changed to either the comparative or superlative form. *Happy* is a positive noun because it can be used to describe a noun, but it can also be changed to *happier* or *happiest* in order to compare things. Since *happy* is a positive adjective that can be changed to *happiest* when more than two happy things are being compared, *happiest* is not a positive adjective. C is incorrect.

Choice D says that *happiest* is a superlative adjective. Superlative adjectives are used to compare three or more nouns. Since each of the thousands of days in John's life are being compared, it is true that more than three nouns are being compared. Again, the suffix *-est* is also used, which shows that this adjective is superlative. D is correct!

EXAMPLE

Choose the word, or words, that best completes the sentence.

Marie's meeting was ____ than Dana's meeting.

a. The most boring
b. More boring
c. Boring
d. Bored

Choice A says that *the most boring* best completes the sentence. In the sentence, one meeting is being compared to another, so only two meetings are being compared. Since choice A uses the word *most*, this choice is a superlative adjective. Superlative adjectives are used to compare three or more nouns, not two. Choice A is incorrect.

Choice B says that *more boring* best completes the sentence. This choice uses the word *more*, instead of *most. More* is used in comparative adjectives to compare two nouns. Since two meetings are being compared in the sentence, the comparative adjective *more boring* is the best choice. B is correct.

Choice C says that *boring* best completes the sentence. The only word in this answer choice is *boring*, which is a positive adjective used to describe a noun. While the sentence suggests that both meetings were boring, the sentence is comparing the two meetings. Positive adjectives are used to describe, not compare, so choice C is incorrect.

Choice D says that *bored* best completes the sentence. Like choice C, *bored* is a positive adjective used to describe a noun. Since positive adjectives without words like *more* or *most* or suffixes like -*er* or -*est* are not used to compare, *bored* is not a good choice for this sentence. *Bored* is also used to describe a state or emotion, so it is not logical to describe a meeting as bored in this sentence. D is incorrect.

ADVERBS

An **adverb** is a word that is used to **modify,** or describe, a verb, adjective, or another adverb. Usually, adverbs answer one of these questions: *When? Where? How?* and *Why?* The negatives *not* and *never* are considered adverbs. Adverbs that modify adjectives or other adverbs **strengthen** or **weaken** the words that they modify.

Examples:

> He walks *quickly* through the crowd.
>
> The water flows *smoothly* on the rocks.

Note: Adverbs are usually indicated by the suffix *-ly*, which has been added to the root word. For instance, *quick* can be made into an adverb by adding *-ly* to construct *quickly*. Some words that end in *-ly* do not follow this rule and can function as other parts of speech. Examples of adjectives ending in *-ly* include: *early, friendly, holy, lonely, silly*, and *ugly*. To know if a word that ends in *-ly* is an adjective or adverb, check your dictionary. Also, while many adverbs end in *-ly*, you need to remember that not all adverbs end in *-ly*.

Examples:

> He is *never* angry.
>
> You are *too* irresponsible to travel alone.

TYPES OF ADVERBS

Different types of adverbs are used to describe particular aspects of a verb, adjective, or other adverb. The following are examples of common types of adverbs:

Time: Some adverbs show when something was done, such as *yesterday*, *today*, or *in two days.*

Manner: Some adverbs show the way something was done, such as *hurriedly*, *neatly*, *grumpily*, or *loudly.*

Frequency: Some adverbs show how often something was done, such as *seldom*, *often*, *never*, or *often*.

Degree: Some adverbs show how much or to what degree something was done, such as *completely*, *barely*, *highly*, or *halfway*.

Conjunctive: Conjunctive adverbs are used similarly to conjunctions, as they connect different ideas, but they can connect ideas from different clauses or sentences. Some examples of conjunctive adverbs are *however*, *alternatively*, *likewise*, and *then*.

COMPARISON WITH ADVERBS

The rules for comparing adverbs are the same as the rules for adjectives.

The **positive** degree is the standard form of an adverb.

> Example: He arrives *soon.* | She speaks *softly* to her friends.

The **comparative** degree compares one person or thing to another person or thing.

> Example: He arrives *sooner* than Sarah. | She speaks *more softly* than him.

The **superlative** degree compares more than two people or things.

> Example: He arrives *soonest* of the group. | She speaks the *most softly* of any of her friends.

Review Video: Adverbs
Visit mometrix.com/academy and enter code: 713951

EXAMPLE

Identify the conjunctive adverb in the following sentences.

> Every night, Savannah's brother loudly gets up to get a glass of water. Consequently, she has started sleeping with earmuffs on so that he does not wake her up at night.

a. Every night
b. Loudly
c. Consequently
d. At night

Choice A says that *every night* is a conjunctive adverb. What does *every night* describe in this sentence? It describes how often Savannah's brother loudly gets a glass of water. This means that *every night* shows the frequency that Savannah's brother does this action. Since *every night* is an adverb that shows frequency, choice A is incorrect.

Choice B says that *loudly* is a conjunctive adverb. In this sentence, what does *loudly* describe? It describes the way that Savannah's brother gets a glass of water each night. This means that *loudly* is an adverb that shows manner. *Loudly* is not a conjunctive adverb, so choice B is incorrect.

Choice C says that *consequently* is a conjunctive adverb. What function does *consequently* have in this sentence? It shows the reason that Savannah started wearing earmuffs while she sleeps. It also shows a connection between the information in the first sentence and the information in the second sentence. Since *consequently* connects the ideas in these sentences, it is a conjunctive adverb. Choice C is correct.

Choice D says that *at night* is a conjunctive adverb. *At* and *night* work together to form an adverbial phrase. Which type of adverb do they form? In this sentence, *at night* shows when Savannah wants to avoid being woken up by her brother. This makes *at night* an adverb that shows time, meaning that *at night* is not a conjunctive adverb and choice D is incorrect.

PREPOSITIONS

A **preposition** is a word placed before a noun or pronoun that shows the relationship between an object and another word in the sentence.

Common prepositions:

about	before	during	on	under
after	beneath	for	over	until
against	between	from	past	up
among	beyond	in	through	with
around	by	of	to	within
at	down	off	toward	without

Examples:

The napkin is *in* the drawer.

The Earth rotates *around* the Sun.

The needle is *beneath* the haystack.

Can you find "me" *among* the words?

PREPOSITIONAL PHRASES

One important thing to know about prepositions is that they form special phrases, called prepositional phrases. A **prepositional phrase** begins with a preposition and ends with a noun or pronoun that is the object of the preposition. Normally, the prepositional phrase functions as an **adjective** or an **adverb** within the sentence.

Examples:

prepositional phrase

The picnic is on the blanket.

prepositional phrase

I am sick with a fever today.

prepositional phrase

Among the many flowers, John found a four-leaf clover.

Be careful not to mistake the object in a prepositional phrase as the subject of a sentence. The subject of the sentence will not be found in a prepositional phrase because a prepositional phrase is used to describe how an object is related to the subject. Prepositional phrases do not influence subject-verb agreement.

Prepositional phrases do not influence subject-verb agreement. For example, consider the following sentence:

The basket (simple subject) of clothes (prepositional phrase) is (verb) on the floor in the laundry room.

This sentence contains a prepositional phrase between the simple subject and the verb. The simple subject is *basket*, which is a singular noun, and the verb is *is*, which is a singular verb. They are separated by the prepositional phrase "of clothes." Even though the plural noun *clothes* comes right before the singular verb *is*, this verb shows the action of the singular noun *basket*.

Review Video: Prepositions
Visit mometrix.com/academy and enter code: 946763

EXAMPLE

Which of the following could NOT complete the sentence?

She went ____ the cave.

a. Sadly
b. Into
c. From
d. Through

Choice A says that the missing word is *sadly*. The blank is between *went* and *the cave*, meaning that the missing word will connect these pieces of the sentence. While *sadly* could be used here to show how the girl felt, there would still be missing information. A preposition is needed here to show whether she entered, exited, or stood outside of the cave. *Sadly* is an adverb, so A is the correct answer.

Choice B says that *into* would complete the sentence. Does *into* complete the sentence without leaving missing information? To say *she went into the cave* is a logical, complete sentence. Choice B is incorrect.

Choice C says that the missing word is *from*. This creates the sentence *she went from the cave*. Since she could have left the cave to go somewhere else, this is also a logical, complete sentence. Choice C is incorrect.

Choice D says that *through* would complete the sentence. The sentence would read *she went through the cave*. Since she could have explored the whole cave or found an exit on the other side of it, *through* can logically complete the sentence. Choice D is incorrect.

EXAMPLE

Identify the prepositional phrase in the following sentence.

Mable visited the store to buy some vegetables.

a. To buy
b. Visited the store
c. The store to buy
d. To buy some vegetables

Remember the pieces of a prepositional phrase. Prepositional phrases should begin with a preposition and end with a noun or pronoun. Considering these rules, can any of the answer choices be eliminated? Choice B and choice C can be eliminated because neither choice begins with a preposition!

That leaves choices A and D. Choice A says that the prepositional phrase is *to buy*. This does start with a preposition, and it does give more information about Mable's trip to the store. However, it does not end with a noun or pronoun. Choice D says that the prepositional phrase is *to buy some vegetables*. Choice D begins with a preposition and ends with a noun, and it explains why Mabel went to the store.

Choice D is the only choice that has all of the pieces of a prepositional phrase, so D is correct!

EXAMPLE

Read the sentence below and answer the following question.

> A band with 15 members _____ performing at my restaurant tonight.

Identify the verb that best completes the sentence.

a. Were
b. Is
c. Are
d. Are not

This question is asking which verb should go in the blank. There are a couple of reasons why choosing the correct verb for this sentence may be confusing. First of all, there are two nouns that appear before the verb. Second, one of these nouns is singular and one is plural.

The first step is to determine which noun goes with the verb. The two nouns are *band* and *members*. While *members* is closest to the blank, it is part of a prepositional phrase that describes *band*. The subject of the sentence is *band*, so the verb must agree with *band*.

Is *band* singular or plural? The sentence says that the band has multiple members, but there is only one band. *Band* is a collective noun, meaning that it is a singular noun. This means that the correct verb will also be singular. With this in mind, can any of the answer choices be eliminated?

Choices A, C, and D are all plural verbs. Even though the blank appears after a plural noun, this noun is part of a prepositional phrase. The verb should match the singular subject *band*. The only choice with a singular verb is choice B, so B is the correct answer.

CONJUNCTIONS

Conjunctions join words, phrases, or clauses and they show the connection between the joined pieces. **Coordinating conjunctions** connect equal parts of sentences. Coordinating conjunctions can also be used to create compound subjects and compound predicates, in addition to compound sentences.

COORDINATING CONJUNCTIONS

The **coordinating conjunctions** include: *and, but, yet, or, nor, for,* and *so*

Compound Subjects:

compound subject
Terry *and* Marissa went to the movies last Saturday.

compund subject
Either pumpkin pie *or* apple pie would be a good dessert to bring to Thanksgiving dinner.

compound subject
Neither the clownfish *nor* the goldfish liked the new fish food very much.

Compound Predicates:

compound predicate
Veronica left school *and* picked up her sister from soccer practice.

compound predicate
The cat did not take a nap *or* play with the dog yesterday.

Compound Sentences:

The rock was small, *but* it was heavy.

She drove in the night, *and* he drove in the day.

Bill dressed nicely today, *for* he must give an important presentation this afternoon.

SUBORDINATING CONJUNCTIONS

Subordinating conjunctions link dependent clauses, clauses with either a subject or a predicate, to independent clauses, clauses with both a subject and a predicate, to form a complex sentence. The subordinating conjunction will always be at the beginning of the dependent clause. When the dependent clause is at the beginning of the sentence, it will end with a comma. When the independent clause is at the beginning of the sentence, no comma is needed.

Common **subordinating conjunctions** include:

after	since	whenever
although	so that	where
because	unless	wherever
before	until	whether
in order that	when	while

Examples:

I am hungry *because* I did not eat breakfast.

He went home *when* everyone left.

While her brother ate dinner, she played his favorite video game.

Review Video: Subordinating Conjunctions
Visit mometrix.com/academy and enter code: 958913

Example

Which of the following is a complex sentence?

a. Joseph went grocery shopping and put all of the groceries away at home.
b. Joseph went grocery shopping, and he put all of the groceries away at home.
c. Joseph went grocery shopping and put all of the groceries away when he got home.
d. Joseph went grocery shopping; he put all of the groceries away at home.

Choice A contains one subject and a compound predicate. Because there is only one subject, Joseph, there is only one clause. Since the sentence is made of one independent clause and a prepositional phrase, it is a simple sentence, and choice A is incorrect.

Choice B contains two clauses. The clauses are separated by a comma and a coordinating conjunction, and both are independent clauses. This sentence contains a prepositional phrase and two independent clauses, so it is a compound sentence. Choice B is incorrect.

Choice C contains two clauses. There are two subjects in the sentence, *Joseph* and *he*. Even though one clause is much shorter than the other, these subjects each go with a different clause. The first clause is independent. The second clause is dependent, as it begins with the word *when*. Since the sentence is made of one independent clause and one dependent clause, it is a complex sentence. Choice C is correct.

Choice D contains two clauses. They are both independent clauses, because they both contain a subject and a predicate, and they both form complete thoughts. Since there is no coordinating conjunction, they are linked by a semicolon. Since the sentence is made from two independent clauses, it is a compound sentence. Choice D is incorrect.

End Punctuation

Periods

Use a period to end all sentences except direct questions and exclamations. Periods are also used for abbreviations.

Examples: 3 p.m. | 2 a.m. | Mr. Jones | Mrs. Stevens | Dr. Smith | Bill, Jr. | Pennsylvania Ave.

Note: An abbreviation is a shortened form of a word or phrase.

Question Marks

Question marks should be used following a **direct question**. A polite request can be followed by a period instead of a question mark.

Direct Question: What is for lunch today? | How are you? | Why is that the answer?

Polite Requests: Can you please send me the item tomorrow. | Will you please walk with me on the track.

Review Video: Question Marks
Visit mometrix.com/academy and enter code: 118471

EXCLAMATION MARKS

Exclamation marks are used after a word group or sentence that shows much feeling or has special importance. Exclamation marks should not be overused. They are saved for proper **exclamatory interjections**.

Example: We're going to the finals! | You have a beautiful car! | "That's crazy!" she yelled.

> **Review Video: Exclamation Points**
> Visit mometrix.com/academy and enter code: 199367

COMMAS

The comma is a punctuation mark that can help you understand connections in a sentence. Not every sentence needs a comma. However, if a sentence needs a comma, you need to put it in the right place. A comma in the wrong place or a missing comma will make a sentence's meaning unclear. These are some of the rules for commas:

Use Case	Example
Before a **coordinating conjunction** joining independent clauses in **compound sentences**	Bob caught three fish, and I caught two fish.
Between **items in a series**	I will bring the turkey, the pie, and the coffee.
After a **dependent clause** that **begins a complex sentence**	Before she left, Ashley turned off all of the lights in her house.
After **transition words**	Consequently, Joel's mother grounded him.
After a **prepositional phrase** at the **beginning of a sentence**	At 10 in the evening, Georgia finally arrived home from work.

> **Review Video: When to Use a Comma**
> Visit mometrix.com/academy and enter code: 786797

EXAMPLE

Identify the sentence that contains an error.

a. While my brother did the dishes I folded the laundry.
b. My brother did the dishes, and I folded the laundry at the same time.
c. I folded the laundry while my brother did the dishes.
d. My brother and I worked on our chores at the same time.

Look over the answer choices. Remember that a sentence's structure depends on the types of clauses in the sentence. Sometimes, punctuation marks are required to properly link clauses, such as when linking a dependent clause followed by an independent clause or linking two independent clauses separated by a coordinating conjunction.

Choice A is a complex sentence, since it contains a dependent clause and an independent clause. Remember that when a dependent clause comes before an independent clause, a comma should follow the dependent clause. When an independent clause comes before a dependent clause, the comma is not needed. In this sentence, which type of clause comes first? The dependent clause comes first, so there is a comma missing in this sentence. This sentence does contain an error, so choice A is correct.

Which type of sentence is choice B? It is a compound sentence because it is made of two independent clauses. These clauses are joined by a comma and a coordinating conjunction.

Remember that if a coordinating conjunction is used to join two independent clauses, a comma must be used immediately after the first clause. Leaving out the comma results in a run-on sentence, and using a comma to join independent clauses without a coordinating conjunction creates a comma splice. The sentence does not contain an error, so choice B is incorrect.

Choice C is another complex sentence. It contains an independent clause followed by a dependent clause. Even though the dependent clause begins with *while*, no comma is needed because the independent clause comes before the dependent clause. This sentence does not contain an error, so choice C is incorrect.

Which type of sentence is choice D? It is a simple sentence because it is made of one independent clause. There are no clauses that need to be connected using conjunctions or commas, so this sentence does not contain an error. Choice D is incorrect.

Quotation Marks

Use quotation marks to close off **direct quotations** of a person's written or spoken words, which are also called **dialogue**. Do not use quotation marks around indirect quotations. An indirect quotation gives someone's message without using the person's exact words. Use **single quotation marks** to close off a quotation inside a quotation.

> **Direct Quote**: Nancy said, "I am waiting for Henry to arrive."
>
> **Indirect Quote**: Henry said that he is going to be late to the meeting.
>
> **Quote inside a Quote**: The teacher asked, "Has everyone read Martin Luther King's 'I Have a Dream' speech?"

Quotation marks should be used around the titles of **short works**: newspaper and magazine articles, poems, short stories, songs, television episodes, and radio programs. Titles of **long works** should be italicized when they are part of a typed composition or underlined when they are part of a handwritten composition.

Examples:

> "Rip Van Winkle" (short story by Washington Irving)
>
> "O Captain! My Captain!" (poem by Walt Whitman)

Review Video: Quotation Marks
Visit mometrix.com/academy and enter code: 884918

Example

Identify the correct place for the first quotation mark in the following sentence.

> After her brother threw a baseball inside, Hallie said, If you ever do that again, I'll tell mom" and took the ball.

a. Before *Hallie*
b. Before *said*
c. Before *if*
d. Before *threw*

Remember that quotation marks are used to identify the words that someone wrote or said. This means that the correct place for quotation marks to go is around the words that were spoken aloud or written. This question asks where the quotation marks should start, which means that the answer will include the first word of dialogue. Consider this as you read each answer choice.

Choice A says the quotation marks should start before *Hallie*. Is *Hallie* the first word of dialogue? No, Hallie is the person saying the dialogue. The words *Hallie said* form the dialogue tag, which tells who said the dialogue and how they said it. Quotes do not include dialogue tags, so dialogue tags should not be inside of quotation marks. Choice A is incorrect.

Choice B says the quotation marks should start before *said*. The word *said* is also part of the dialogue tag. The dialogue tag should go right before the first quotation mark or right after the last one, but it should not be within the quotation marks. Choice B is incorrect.

Choice C says the quotation marks should start before *if*. In this sentence, *if* is the first word spoken by Hallie, which makes it the first word of dialogue. Remember that the first quotation mark should go right before the first word of the quote. This means that choice C is correct!

Choice D says the quotation marks should start before *threw*. *Threw* is not part of the quotation, so it is certainly not the first word of dialogue. Choice D is incorrect.

EXAMPLE

Choose the sentence that contains a correctly punctuated title.

a. Edgar Allan Poe wrote many poems and short stories, such as *The Raven* and *The Black Cat*.
b. *Great Expectations* is her favorite novel.
c. I think "Romeo and Juliet" is William Shakespeare's most well-known play.
d. "The Great Gatsby" is a novel that has been made into multiple movies.

Choice A contains two titles in italics. Titles of long, or major, works should be italicized. This sentence includes the title of a poem and a short story. Both of these are short, or minor, works, so they should be in quotation marks rather than italics. Choice A is incorrect.

Choice B contains one title in italics. Remember that italics are for major works. The title in this sentence is the title of a novel, which is a major work. The title in this sentence is appropriately punctuated, so choice B is correct.

Choice C contains a title in quotation marks. Quotation marks should be used for titles of short, or minor, works. This sentence includes the title of a play. Plays are considered major works, so this title should be italicized. Choice C is incorrect.

Choice D contains one title in quotation marks. This is the title of a novel, so it is the title of a major work. The title should be italicized, but it is in quotation marks. Choice D is incorrect.

Apostrophes

An apostrophe is used to show **possession** or the **deletion of letters in contractions**. An apostrophe is not needed with the possessive pronouns *his, hers, its, ours, theirs, whose*, and *yours*.

Singular Nouns: David's car | a book's theme | my brother's board game

Plural Nouns that end with -*s*: the scissors' handle | boys' basketball

Plural Nouns that end without -*s*: Men's department | the people's adventure

Review Video: Apostrophes
Visit mometrix.com/academy and enter code: 213068

Review Video: Punctuation Errors in Possessive Pronouns
Visit mometrix.com/academy and enter code: 221438

Apostrophes in Contractions

Contractions are combinations of words. Contractions involve taking two words, removing at least one letter from one of the words, putting an apostrophe in its place, and removing the space. For example, *does not* can be written as the contraction *doesn't*. The *o* is removed from *not* and is replaced with an apostrophe, which represents the removed letter, so it appears as *n't*. The space after does is then removed, turning *does not* into the contraction *doesn't*. Some more examples of contractions are listed below.

First Word	Second Word	Contraction
Can	Not	Can't
Do	Not	Don't
She	Will	She'll
They	Will	They'll
He	Is	He's
It	Is	It's
They	Are	They're
I	Am	I'm

Not all words can be used to form contractions, but many small, commonly used words can.

Capitalization

One important part of using correct grammar is properly capitalizing words. Usually, only nouns will be capitalized, but there are some exceptions. The most important capitalization rule is that the first word of every sentence, no matter what part of speech it is, should be capitalized. Another exception is that the pronoun *I* should always be capitalized.

Proper nouns are always capitalized, but sometimes it can be tricky to decide whether or not a noun is a proper noun. Some words that are usually common nouns may become proper nouns when used with other words or phrases. Also, when words that are not nouns are used with a noun, or when a group of words are used together as one noun, those words may also need to be capitalized.

Titles of Books, Stories, and Essays

Most of the words in titles of things like books, stories, and essays should be capitalized, but some should not. The very first word in a title should always be capitalized. Any other word in a title that is a noun, pronoun, adjective, verb or adverb should be capitalized. Articles, such as *a* or *the*, should not be capitalized. Short conjunctions and prepositions are usually not capitalized.

Abbreviations, Initials, and Acronyms

Abbreviations are shortened versions of other words. When an abbreviation shortens, or abbreviates, a word that should be capitalized, the abbreviation's first letter should also be capitalized. When the shortened word is a noun that is not capitalized, the abbreviation should be in lowercase. Initials are usually written using the first letter from multiple words. For example, John Fitzgerald Kennedy is commonly referred to by his initials, JFK. Acronyms also use the first letter from multiple words, but they are different from initials because they form words on their own. For example, NASA is an acronym for National Aeronautics and Space Administration. Some acronyms, like NASA, omit small words, such as *and*, *of*, and *for*. When initials and acronyms are used for proper nouns, each letter should be capitalized.

The types of words and phrases in the chart below are proper nouns and should always be capitalized:

	Description	Example
Historical Periods	A range of time in history that is related to specific events or circumstances	During the Romantic Period, many authors and poets wrote about their emotions.
Historical Events	Names of important events that happened in history	Napoleon Bonaparte led France after the French Revolution.
Historical Documents	Titles of important papers or compositions that are connected to historical events	The Mayflower Compact was written to create rules and expectations for the colony in Plymouth.
Languages	Names of the different languages that people speak	I want to learn to speak Cantonese, Spanish, and German.
Races and Ethnicities	Words often used to describe a person's heritage or cultural group	Malia taught her granddaughter how to hula so she could share a tradition of her Native Hawaiian heritage with her.
Nationalities	Words that describe which country a person is from	My teacher who moved to Canada last year is Romanian.
Organizations	Titles of official groups formed by people	Fewer than half of the states in America have a team in the National Basketball Association.

Review Video: Capitalization in Grammar
Visit mometrix.com/academy and enter code: 369678

Example

Identify the capitalization mistake in the following sentences.

> My brother and I want to open a bakery, so we discussed what we should call it. I wanted to give it a name that would form the acronym Bake, but we couldn't think of a good name using those letters. My brother suggested Bakery Brothers and said that if we ever need to abbreviate the name, we can call it Bakery Bros. or BB.

a. All of the letters in *Bake* should be capitalized.
b. *Bakery Brothers* should be in lowercase.
c. All of the letters in *Bros.* should be capitalized.
d. The second *B* in *BB* should be lowercase.

There are three types of abbreviations in these sentences. The second sentence contains an acronym, and the third sentence contains a shortened word and an initialism. Consider the different capitalization rules for each of these to identify the error in the sentences.

Choice A says that all of the letters in *Bake* should be capitalized. Even though *bake* is a verb that usually should not be capitalized at all, it is used as an acronym in this sentence. That means that each letter should be capitalized, so choice A is correct.

Choice B says that all of the letters in *Bakery Brothers* should be in lowercase. In the sentences, *Bakery Brothers* is the full name of the bakery. Since it is the name of a place, *Bakery Brothers* is a proper noun. It is correctly capitalized, so choice B is incorrect.

Choice C says that all of the letters in *Bros.* should be capitalized. *Bros.* is a shortening of *brothers.* Remember that shortened words should follow the same capitalization rules as the original word. Since the first letter of *brothers* is capitalized in the phrase *Bakery Brothers*, *Bros.* is written correctly. Choice C is incorrect.

Choice D says that the second *B* in *BB* should be in lowercase. *BB* is an initialism that takes the first letter from each word in the name *Bakery Brothers.* Remember that all of the letters in initialisms must be capitalized, so *BB* is correctly capitalized. Choice D is incorrect.

Example

Choose the correctly capitalized organization name.

a. National Association for People who Hate Taking Naps
b. Organization for The Most Interesting People in America
c. Club for High-School Students Who love Reading
d. Nebraskan Club for Mountain Climbers

Names of organizations follow the same capitalization rules as titles. Remember that when capitalizing titles, it is important to consider each word's part of speech. Nouns, pronouns, verbs, adjectives, and adverbs are always capitalized in titles. Consider the part of speech of every word in each answer choice.

In choice A, the capitalized words include adjectives, nouns, and verbs. These words are all correctly capitalized. *For* and *who* are in lowercase. Which parts of speech are these words? *For* is a preposition. Remember that short prepositions are not usually capitalized in titles, so leaving *for* in lowercase is acceptable. *Who* is a pronoun. Pronouns should always be capitalized in titles, so this is an error. Choice A is incorrect.

In choice B, there is an incorrectly capitalized word. An article should not be capitalized in a title unless it is the first word in the title. In this choice, *the* is capitalized in the middle of the title. This is an error, so choice B is incorrect.

In choice C, each capitalized word is correct. These words include nouns, adjectives, a pronoun, and a verb. *For* and *love* are in lowercase. Since *for* is a short preposition, it is acceptable to leave it in lowercase. However, *love* is a verb in this title. Verbs must be capitalized in titles, so this is an error. Choice C is incorrect.

In choice D, the capitalized words include adjectives and nouns. Words belonging to these parts of speech should always be capitalized in titles. The only word that is in lowercase is *for*, which may be left in lowercase because it is a short preposition. All of the words in this organization name are correctly capitalized or left in lowercase, so choice D is correct!

Chapter Quiz

1. Every sentence always has a subject and a/an:

a. Imperative
b. Preposition
c. Predicate
d. Modifier

2. Which of the following sentences does NOT have an implied subject?

a. Take John on a quick walk.
b. Don't get lost.
c. John knows the way to the park.
d. Bring me back some flowers.

3. Which pronoun can be either singular or plural depending on what it is representing in the context of the sentence?

a. Nobody
b. Either
c. Several
d. All

4. Which of the following is written in third person perspective?

a. I am walking
b. He is walking
c. You are walking
d. We are walking

5. Which of the following best describes the function of an indirect object?

a. Shows how an action had an influence
b. Takes or receives the action of a verb
c. Explains or describes the subject
d. Shows that there is more information needed

6. Which of the following is a group of words that contains both a subject and a verb, and can be either independent or dependent?

a. Antecedent
b. Fragment
c. Phrase
d. Clause

7. Which of the following is an example of a complex sentence (as opposed to a simple or compound sentence)?

a. The time has come, and we are ready.
b. Judy and Alan watered the lawn and pulled weeds.
c. Marcia got married after she finished college.
d. I woke up at dawn; the sun was just coming up.

8. What method of correcting run-on sentences is the easiest way to make the sentence correct and more interesting at the same time?

a. Split into separate sentences
b. Join clauses properly
c. Reduce to one clause with a compound verb
d. Make one clause dependent

9. Which of the following is a word placed before a noun or pronoun that shows the relationship between an object and another word in the sentence?

a. Adjective
b. Adverb
c. Preposition
d. Conjunction

10. Which of the following should be put in single quotation marks?

a. Quote inside a quote
b. Indirect quote
c. Direct quote
d. All of the above

Chapter Quiz Answer Key

1. C: See section **Predicates**

2. C: See section **Subjects**

3. D: See section **Depend on Context**

4. B: See section **Person Agreement Examples**

5. A: See section **Indirect Objects**

6. D: See section **Clauses**

7. C: See section **Complex**

8. D: See section **Run-on Sentences**

9. C: See section **Prepositions**

10. A: See section **Quotation Marks**

Written Essay

Essays

Essays usually focus on one topic, subject, or goal. There are several types of essays, including informative, persuasive, and narrative. An essay's structure and formality depend on the type of essay and its goal. While narrative essays typically do not include outside sources, other types of essays often require some research and the use of primary and secondary sources.

The basic format of an essay typically has three major parts: the introduction, the body, and the conclusion. The body is further divided into the writer's main points. Most essays will have at least three main points, but essays that go into more depth can have almost any number of main points.

An essay's introduction should answer three questions:

1. What is the **subject** of the essay?

   If an essay is about a book, the answer would include the title and author of the book, as well as any additional information needed, such as the subject or argument of the book.

2. How does the essay **discuss** the subject?

   To answer this, the writer briefly summarizes the main points and the evidence supporting them to let readers know how the essay is organized and what information they can expect to read.

3. What will the essay **prove**?

   This information is in the thesis statement, usually the opening paragraph's last sentence, which clearly states the writer's message.

The body elaborates on all the main points related to the thesis, introducing one main point at a time, and includes supporting evidence with each main point. Each body paragraph should state the point in a topic sentence, which is usually the first sentence in the paragraph. The paragraph should then explain the point's meaning, support it with quotations or other evidence, and then explain how this point and the evidence are related to the thesis. The writer should then repeat this procedure in a new paragraph for each additional main point.

The conclusion restates the content of the introduction, including the thesis, to remind the reader of the essay's main argument or subject. The essay writer may also summarize the highlights of the argument or description contained in the body of the essay, following the same organization originally used in the body. For example, a conclusion might look like: Point 1 + Point 2 + Point 3 = Thesis, or Point 1 → Point 2 → Point 3 → Thesis Proof. Good organization makes essays easier for writers to compose and provides a guide for readers to follow. Well-organized essays hold attention better and are more likely to get readers to believe or agree with the writer.

Using Sources in Essays

Sometimes writers use information from others in their work. This is most common in expository and persuasive writing. For an expository essay, a writer may not know all of the information that he or she needs to finish the composition. The writer may use other people's work to find the missing information and complete the composition. Persuasive writers may do research to find facts or statements from others that support their own beliefs and make their writing more persuasive. In both cases, research helps the writer find information that **supports** his or her **original work**.

Outside information must be relevant, true, and helpful to be appropriate for a composition. Writers must also be careful not to use too much outside information, since this can make the composition unoriginal. If a writer does use outside information, it is extremely important that the writer mention in the composition where the information came from. If the writer forgets or chooses not to say where the information came from, he or she has stolen someone else's work and presented it as their own. Doing this is called **plagiarism**.

INFORMATIONAL TEXTS

Informational texts, also called instructional or expository texts, are compositions written to inform the reader about a specific topic. An informational essay can inform readers in a variety of ways, such as giving them instructions, telling them facts about the topic, or teaching them why something happens. Informational texts should be logical, meaning that they should present information in an order that the reader can easily understand, and they should include the right amount of information so the writer successfully informs his or her audience of new information.

Informational texts should also focus on a **controlling idea**. In the introduction of an informational text, there may be a sentence or two that clearly state the essay's controlling idea. This sentence, or sentences, is called a **thesis statement**. The controlling idea should be clear throughout the composition. By emphasizing the controlling idea in the introduction, body, and conclusion, the writer can ensure that the controlling idea is clear. One way to make sure that the controlling idea is emphasized is to think about the purpose of each part of the essay. The introduction prepares the reader by telling them what the rest of the essay is about, so the controlling idea should be **introduced** in this section. The body tells the reader the information the writer wants to tell the audience, so this **explains** the controlling idea and facts about it to the reader. The conclusion is used to **remind** the reader of how the information in the body is related and **restates** the controlling idea one final time.

Review Video: Informational Text
Visit mometrix.com/academy and enter code: 924964

STRUCTURES OR ORGANIZATIONAL PATTERNS IN INFORMATIONAL TEXTS

Informational text can be **descriptive**, meaning that it gives information that can be experienced through the five senses, or it answers the questions what, who, when, where, and why. One common method of organizing informational text is to put it in a certain sequence, or order. **Chronological** texts include events in the order that they occurred, from start to finish. **How-to**, or **instructional**, texts organize information into a series of instructions in the order in which the steps should be followed. **Comparison-contrast** structures of informational text describe different ideas to their readers by pointing out how things or ideas are similar and how they are different. **Cause and effect** structures of informational text describe events that occurred and the causes or reasons for those events. **Problem and solution** structures of informational texts introduce and describe problems and offer one or more solutions for each problem described.

ARGUMENTATIVE WRITING

In argumentative writing, the writer expresses a belief or opinion that he or she wants to lead readers to agree with. This writing is also refered to as persuasive writing since the author is trying to persuade the reader to believe a certain belief. When writing an argumentative composition, the writer should first identify the **topic** his or her opinion is about. The topic may be serious or fun, as long as there is one clear topic in the composition. The next step is for the writer to determine his or her opinion on the topic and determine why he or she holds that opinion. In order to persuade others to agree with their opinion, the writer must be able to give readers reasons to support the opinion. If the writer does not know why he or she has an opinion, it will be difficult to convince readers to agree. In addition to having reasons that support their opinion, writers should prepare examples that support each of these reasons in order to strengthen their composition.

Once the writer has determined his or her topic, opinion, and reasons for having the opinion, he or she is ready to begin writing an argumentative essay. In the introduction, the writer should capture the reader's interest, introduce the topic, and reveal his or her opinion about the topic. In the body of the composition, the writer should remind the reader of the opinion and give his or her reasons for holding the opinion. If the writer has any examples, facts, or other information that supports his or her opinion or reasons for believing it, these should also be included in the body. Writers may also use a body paragraph to mention opposing opinions or beliefs and explain why they disagree with them. As in other compositions, the conclusion should remind the reader of the essay's topic and purpose, as well as remind the reader how the opinion has been explained and supported. The conclusion should also invite the reader to continue thinking about the topic and writer's opinion. This can be done through questions or statements that lead readers to consider whether or not they agree with the author's opinion or what their own opinions are.

Review Video: Argumentative Writing
Visit mometrix.com/academy and enter code: 561544

INFORMATIVE VS. PERSUASIVE WRITING

Informative writing, also called explanatory or expository writing, is written to show that something is true or factual, while **persuasive** writing is written to lead the reader to agree with something that may or may not be true or factual. While persuasive text is written to **persuade** readers to agree with the author's position, informative text simply **provides information** to readers. Informative writing **informs** readers about why or how something is as it is. This can include offering new information, explaining how a process works, or describing a concept for readers.

Facts and Opinions

Writers and readers must always be aware of the difference between fact and opinion. A **fact** can be tested and proven to be true. An **opinion**, on the other hand, is someone's personal thoughts or feelings. Opinions are often not changed by information. If an author writes that a newborn elephant is about five times taller than a newborn giraffe, then he or she is stating a fact. If the author writes that giraffes are more interesting than elephants, then he or she is giving an opinion because this cannot be proven to be true or false. Opinions are often supported by facts. For instance, the author might use a comparison between the way that giraffes eat and the way elephants eat as evidence of how giraffes are more interesting. An opinion supported by facts tends to be more convincing. On the other hand, when authors support their opinions with other opinions, readers should seriously think about and read the argument carefully to see whether it is logical and trustworthy.

Review Video: Distinguishing Fact and Opinion
Visit mometrix.com/academy and enter code: 870899

Responding to a Text

An essay prompt may require writers to write about a text they have read. When writing an essay like this, writers should show that they understand the text they have read. They may mention their own thoughts, ideas, and opinions in the essay. However, the main idea of the essay should be about the text mentioned in the prompt.

When planning the essay, writers should consider what the text is about and how it is written. Writers should identify the purpose, main idea, and structure of the text. For informational and persuasive texts, they should also think about the supporting details the author used in the text. All of these facts about the text will help writers understand the text well and allow the writer to create a response to the text.

Responding to Multiple Texts

Essay prompts may ask writers to write about more than one text. In this case, writers should identify the purpose, main idea, and structure of each text. They should also look at the kinds of supporting details that the author of each text uses. Once writers know these details, they should think about the differences and similarities between the texts. The main ideas of each text may oppose each other, or one may support the other. Writers will need to write about both texts in the essay, so they must understand both texts and the connection between the texts.

Chapter Quiz

1. What type of essay does NOT typically include outside sources?

a. Expository
b. Informative
c. Persuasive
d. Narrative

2. Which of the following is NOT true of informational texts?

a. Informational texts are also called instructional or expository texts
b. Informational texts should be logical
c. Informational texts should focus on a central idea
d. Informational texts can only be structured chronologically

3. In an argumentative essay, which of the following should be included in the body?

a. A reminder of the writer's opinion and his or her reasons for holding the opinion
b. Examples, facts, or other information that supports the writer's opinion
c. Opposing opinions or beliefs and explanations of why the writer disagrees with them
d. All of the above

Chapter Quiz Answer Key

1. D: See section **Essays**

2. D: See section **Structures or Organizational Patterns in Informational Texts**

3. D: See section **Argumentative Writing**

Informational Text Example

Below is a prompt for an informational text. There is also an example of an essay that addresses the prompt. There are multiple drafts of this essay to show what kinds of changes a writer may make during the writing process to improve his or her work.

Prompt:

One of the things that makes each person unique is the hobbies they enjoy doing in their free time. Write about a hobby you enjoy. Be sure to include information about how you became interested in the hobby.

Rough Draft

Prepare to see your boredom disappear before your very eyes! Presto! That is what my favorite hobby did for me. Learning and performing magic tricks for my friends and family is my favorite hobby.

Every time we go to my grandparents' house, he does a card trick when we get there. Last year on my birthday, he gave me a cool deck of cards and showed me how to do a trick. I practiced it a couple of times and then tried it with some of my friends. I did it correctly with most of them, and they were so impressed! I was looking up new card tricks online when I discovered that there are other kinds of magic tricks, too. I decided to learn one to show my grandpa the next time he visited. I ended up learning five tricks that day! Since then, learning magic tricks has been my hobby.

Before I started learning magic tricks, my hobby was collecting rocks. I started collecting rocks around my neighborhood, but then I also started collecting them on vacations. I enjoyed that hobby until school started again. Then I had fewer opportunities to find cool rocks. I enjoy learning magic tricks much more, and it is something I can do any day after school. I also like learning magic tricks more that collecting things because it is more exciting. Looking at the rocks I had collected got old, but I never get tired of magic tricks!

One of my favorite things about my hobby is that I can perform magic shows. Once I have learned several new magic tricks, I get to do a magic show for my parents and my sister. If there was ever a talent show at school, I would do magic tricks as my talent. It is fun to show off the tricks I have learned, but my favorite part of doing magic shows is seeing that others enjoy my magic tricks. I love that I can share my hobby with others!

I am very thankful to my grandpa for inspiring my hobby! I believe I will always love doing magic tricks and hope I can become a better magician if I keep learning and practicing!

REVISED DRAFT

Prepare to see your boredom disappear before your very eyes! Presto! That is what my favorite hobby did for me. Learning and performing magic tricks for my friends and family is my favorite hobby.

Every time we go to my grandparents' house, he does a card trick when we get there. Last year on my birthday, he gave me a cool deck of cards and showed me how to do a trick. I practiced it a couple of times and then tried it with some of my friends. I did it correctly with most of them, and they were so impressed! I was looking up new card tricks online when I discovered that there are other kinds of magic tricks, too. I decided to learn one to show my grandpa the next time he visited. I ended up learning five tricks that day! Since then, learning magic tricks has been my hobby.

~~Before I started learning magic tricks, my hobby was collecting rocks. I started collecting rocks around my neighborhood, but then I also started collecting them on vacations. I enjoyed that hobby until school started again. Then I had fewer opportunities to find cool rocks. I enjoy learning magic tricks much more, and it is something I can do any day after school. I also like learning magic tricks more that collecting things because it is more exciting. Looking at the rocks I had collected got old, but I never get tired of magic tricks!~~

One of my favorite things about my hobby is that I can perform magic shows. Once I have learned several new magic tricks, I get to do a magic show for my parents and my sister. If there was ever a talent show at school, I would do magic tricks as my talent. It is fun to show off the tricks I have learned, but my favorite part of doing magic shows is seeing that others enjoy my magic tricks. I love that I can share my hobby with others!

I still enjoy watching others do magic tricks, but I enjoy learning and performing them even more. I am very thankful to my grandpa for inspiring my hobby! I believe I will always love doing magic tricks and hope I can become a better magician if I keep learning and practicing!

Revised Draft Notes

Remember the purpose of the revising stage of the writing process. When revising, it is important to look at the whole composition. Do all of the paragraphs strengthen the composition? Do the introduction and conclusion help the reader understand the controlling idea and main points?

First, look at the underlined words. These are words that have been added. In the conclusion, a sentence has been added. This sentence strengthens the composition because it creates a transition from the body to the conclusion. It also gives the writer's thoughts about the details he or she included in the essay. Before, the conclusion began abruptly and only mentioned one of the writer's points from the body of the composition. After this sentence was added, the conclusion became about each of the writer's points from the body paragraphs. This sentence reminds the reader of the writer's points and the composition's controlling idea, instead of focusing on only one of the writer's points.

Next, look at what has been crossed out in this essay. These are words that have been removed. A whole paragraph has been omitted! Why is that? There were no huge errors, and the writing made sense. The paragraph talks about why learning magic tricks is better than the writer's former hobby. While this is related to the controlling idea, this information is not entirely relevant and does not offer much new information about magic tricks. This paragraph does not strengthen the composition or help the reader understand the controlling idea. The writer made a wise choice to remove this information and should later replace it with a paragraph that gives the reader new information about the writer's hobby, why the writer enjoys it, or something the writer has experienced through it.

EDITED DRAFT

Prepare to see your boredom disappear before your very eyes! Presto! ~~That is what my favorite hobby did for me.~~ Learning and performing magic tricks for my friends and family is my favorite hobby.

My interest in magic tricks was inspired by my grandpa. Every time we go to my grandparents' house, he does a card trick when we get there. Last year on my birthday, he gave me a cool deck of cards and showed me how to do a trick. I practiced it a couple of times and then tried it with some of my friends. I did it correctly with most of them, and they were so impressed! I was looking up new card tricks online when I discovered that there are other kinds of magic tricks, too. I decided to learn one to show my grandpa the next time he visited. I ended up learning five tricks that day! Since then, learning magic tricks has been my hobby.

~~Before I started learning magic tricks, my hobby was collecting rocks. I started collecting rocks around my neighborhood, but then I also started collecting them on vacations. I enjoyed that hobby until school started again. Then I had fewer opportunities to find cool rocks. I enjoy learning magic tricks much more, and it is something I can do any day after school. I also like learning magic tricks more that collecting things because it is more exciting. Looking at the rocks I had collected got old, but I never get tired of magic tricks!~~

One of my favorite things about my hobby is that I can perform magic shows. Once I have learned several new magic tricks, I get to do a magic show for my parents and my sister. ~~If there was ever a talent show at school, I would do magic tricks as my talent.~~ My sister wants me to do a magic show at her birthday party. I am so excited to do my magic tricks for a new audience! It is fun to show off the tricks I have learned, but my favorite part of doing magic shows is seeing that others enjoy my magic tricks. I love that I can share my hobby with others!

I still enjoy watching others do magic tricks, but I enjoy learning and performing them even more. I am very thankful to my grandpa for inspiring my hobby! I believe I will always love doing magic tricks and hope I can become a better magician if I keep learning and practicing!

Edited Draft Notes

Since the writer has revised his or her work, the next step is to edit the composition. Remember that editing is very similar to revising, but editing usually includes paying attention to each paragraph, instead of the whole composition. Look at the changes that were made to each paragraph.

In the introduction, a sentence was removed. Why was it removed? While it said something about hobbies, it did not strengthen the composition. This sentence connects the hook to the prompt, but it does not introduce the topic or give the reader useful information. This sentence is not about the specific hobby being discussed in the composition. While it gives a transition from the hook to the thesis, a different sentence would better prepare the reader for the information in the rest of the essay.

Only one change has been made in the second paragraph. A transition has been added to the beginning of the first sentence. This helps connect this paragraph to the rest of the composition and prepares the reader for the information in the paragraph. Before, this paragraph simply described an event and explained how it led the writer to begin his or her hobby. However, the reader is not told why the paragraph is relevant until later in the paragraph. Now, the reader is told the purpose at the beginning of the paragraph. This strengthens the composition by improving how this paragraph flows with the rest of the essay.

What has been changed in the fourth paragraph? Another sentence has been crossed out, and two new ones have been added. Why? This paragraph tells why the writer enjoys doing magic shows, and it includes the example of magic shows the writer has performed for his or her family. The end of the paragraph tells the reasons why the writer has enjoyed doing the magic shows. The crossed-out sentence tells the reader that the author would do a magic act for a school talent show. This detail is relevant to the rest of the paragraph, but it does not support the paragraph's main point. The underlined sentences include supporting details that explain that the writer has an opportunity to do a show for a new audience. This example is better because it elaborates on the first example and connects the examples to the reason the writer enjoys doing magic shows. These sentences help the paragraph flow better and support the other ideas in the paragraph.

The remaining marks are left to remind the writer that the third paragraph still needs to be replaced. This information will be added before the final draft is finished.

FINAL DRAFT

Prepare to see your boredom disappear before your very eyes! Presto! That is what happened to me when I began learning how to do magic tricks. Now, learning and performing magic tricks for my friends and family is my favorite hobby.

My interest in magic tricks was inspired by my grandpa. Every time we go to my grandparents' house, he does a card trick when we get there. Last year on my birthday, he gave me a cool deck of cards and showed me how to do a trick. I practiced it a couple of times and then tried it with some of my friends. I did it correctly with most of them, and they were so impressed! I was looking up new card tricks online when I discovered that there are other kinds of magic tricks, too. I decided to learn one to show my grandpa the next time he visited. I ended up learning five tricks that day! Since then, magic tricks have been my hobby.

While doing magic tricks is very fun, it takes practice at first. Some tricks are difficult to get the hang of because you have to do some steps very carefully. For example, for some tricks, you have to hide a small object in your hand or behind your hand. If the object is not completely hidden or if you make it too obvious that you are hiding something, the trick does not work as well. These tricks are very difficult for me to learn, so I have to practice them more than other tricks. Sometimes it takes patience, but mastering a trick is so fun that practicing is worth it!

One of my favorite things about my hobby is that I can perform magic shows. Once I have learned several new magic tricks, I get to do a magic show for my parents and my sister. My sister wants me to do a magic show at her birthday party. I am so excited to do my magic tricks for a new audience! It is fun to show off the tricks I have learned, but my favorite part of doing magic shows is seeing that others enjoy my magic tricks. I love that I can share my hobby with others!

I still enjoy watching others do magic tricks, but I enjoy learning and performing them even more. I am very thankful to my grandpa for inspiring my hobby! I believe I will always love doing magic tricks and hope I can become a better magician if I keep learning and practicing!

Final Draft Notes

This is the final draft! In this draft, information has been added to the introduction, and there is a new paragraph. Now, the introduction includes a sentence that introduces the controlling idea of the composition and prepares the reader for the information in the rest of the essay. The new paragraph also gives new information about doing magic tricks. This paragraph describes a lesson the writer learned through doing magic tricks and gives the reader more information about the writer's experience practicing the hobby. These additions strengthen the composition by replacing weaker information with details that are more informative and engaging for the reader.

Evaluation

The essay answers the prompt and is on topic throughout the composition. The controlling idea is clear and is stated in the introduction, supported in the body, and restated in the conclusion. The thesis statement restates parts of the prompt and gives the reader a preview of the rest of the essay. The body uses well-structured paragraphs to explain the supporting details and examples and connects them to the controlling idea. The conclusion also emphasizes the controlling idea and supporting details and invites the reader to consider what they have read.

The essay is also interesting and written with a variety of sentence types. It uses transitions and good paragraph structure to make the essay easy for the reader to understand. The introduction also uses a hook to get the reader's attention and help him or her relate to the information in the essay. Not only does this essay answer the prompt and have appropriate structure, but it also makes use of good, engaging, and interesting details.

Reading Practice Test #1

Questions 1–8 pertain to the following passage:

A Garden in the Desert

(1) Barry lives one street up and four houses down from his best friend, Manolo. Barry, his parents, and his older brother Ricardo have lived in the small ranch house for as long as he can remember. Manolo's family moved into their house a few months before Manolo was born. At that time, 10 years ago, their housing development was only five square blocks. About 250 small, one-story houses dotted the streets. Today their housing development is three times as big, and is considered an actual neighborhood. It is called Cypress Heights.

(2) There are no cypresses or any other kinds of trees in Cypress Heights. The neighborhood was built near a desert. It has no heights and no hills – just flat stretches of paved road and concrete sidewalks. Grass sprouts up between the cracks in the sidewalks, but refuses to take root on lawns. Flowers also have a hard time growing in Barry and Manolo's hot and dusty neighborhood. The only plants that grow around most of the houses are patches of ragged-looking weeds.

(3) In contrast to the dusty lawns, most of the ranch houses are very well kept. The outsides of the houses are freshly painted, and many lawns are decorated with bird baths and patio furniture. The lack of gardens and lawns, however, makes the neighborhood look dusty, downtrodden, and old. Without grass roots to knit a protective net in the soil, the wind picks up dirt and blows it all over the roads, roofs, and sidewalks. After a windy day, everything in Cypress Heights is covered in brown and gray dust.

(4) Manolo and Barry love living in Cypress Heights because their houses are so close, and each boy can easily get to the other's house. A short fence surrounds Manolo's backyard. Manolo can jump over the fence and walk along the path in the neighbor's backyard to Barry's street. From there, Manolo can walk past three houses to get to Barry's. The fence around Barry's backyard is too high to jump over and too smooth to climb, so Barry has to stick to the streets to get to Manolo's house.

(5) One summer day, Barry rode his bike over to Manolo's house. He brought a backpack with a picnic lunch.

(6) "Let's go to the playground at the school," said Barry. "I have two peanut butter and jelly sandwiches and two juice boxes for lunch. We can stay there all afternoon."

(7) "Sounds good," said Manolo. His older sister was watching him while his mother was at work. He asked his sister, Rosa, for permission.

(8) "Just be back before five o'clock," said Rosa. "Mom should be home by then."

(9) Barry and Manolo's school was about a mile away. It was a long, brown, one-story building with big windows and a large play set in the front. In the back were two sets of train tracks. Usually, the trains only ran at night, but every so often a freight train would pass the school during the day, making the windows rattle and the children rush from their seats to watch it.

(10) On their way to the schoolyard, they passed a house that had just been sold a few weeks earlier. On the yard, instead of dusty weeds, was white gravel. Dotted around the lawn were different cactus plants. Barry and Manolo stopped their bikes and stared at the lawn.

(11) "It looks great," said Barry. "But I don't want cactus plants in my yard. What if I ran into one while playing tag? That would hurt!"

(12) "There are other plants that work in this area," said a voice from behind a large cactus.

(13) A woman with short brown hair stepped out from behind the cactus and walked over to Barry and Manolo. She had a wide-brimmed hat on her head.

(14) "We planted cacti because they don't need much water," said the woman with a smile. She waved her hand toward her house. "It is too expensive to water plants or a lawn. But there are other drought-resistant plants that will do well here."

(15) "What kind of plant is 'drought resistant'?" asked Manolo.

(16) "Basically, it is a plant that doesn't need much water," said the woman. "They include plants like lavender, aloe, lamb's ear, and oriental yew. I have some of those in pots ready to be planted. If you promise to take care of them, I can give you some to plant in your yards."

(17) "Sure!" said Barry and Manolo at once.

(18) The woman motioned to the boys to follow her behind her house. She put several small plants in a low, flat box attached to the back of her bicycle. She strapped down the plants and climbed on the seat.

(19) "Lead the way," she said.

(20) "Thank you," said Barry. "By the way, I'm Barry and this is Manolo."

(21) "I'm Mrs. Juarez," said the woman. "Nice to meet you."

(22) "Wait a minute," said Barry. "You just moved in. Shouldn't we give presents to you?"

(23) "That's okay," laughed Mrs. Juarez. "I don't have any more room in my garden, so you are doing me a favor by taking them. But, I will take cookies if you have them!"

(24) "Sounds good," said Barry. The three of them headed towards the boys' houses, ready to break ground on their new gardens.

1. Part A: What is the main objective of paragraphs 2 and 3?

a. To describe Manolo's house
b. To describe Barry's house
c. To describe Manolo's and Barry's friendship
d. To describe Manolo's and Barry's neighborhood

Part B: Which sentence best supports your answer?

a. "A short fence surrounds Manolo's backyard."
b. "Manolo's family moved into their house a few months before Manolo was born."
c. "There are no cypresses or any other kinds of trees in Cypress Heights."
d. "From there, Manolo can walk past three houses to get to Barry's."

2. What is strange about the name of Barry's and Manolo's neighborhood: Cypress Heights?

a. There are no Cypress trees and the land is flat
b. The trees in Cypress Heights are actually oak and maple trees
c. Cypress Heights is located in a valley
d. There is no such thing as a Cypress tree

3. Which sentence in paragraph 3 showed that Cypress Heights residents care about how their houses look?

a. "The outsides of the houses are freshly painted, and many lawns are decorated with bird baths and patio furniture."
b. "The lack of gardens and lawns, however, makes the neighborhood look dusty, downtrodden, and old."
c. "Without grass roots to knit a protective net in the soil, the wind picks up dirt and blows it all over the roads, roofs, and sidewalks."
d. "After a windy day, everything in Cypress Heights is covered in brown and gray dust."

4. Why do Barry and Manolo like living close to each other?

a. Because it is convenient for them to visit each other
b. Because Barry's fence is too high to climb
c. Because their bikes don't work
d. Because Manolo has a shorter walk

5. What are "drought-resistant" plants?

a. Plants that can live in very hot climates
b. Plants that can live in very cold climates
c. Plants that can live in very dry climates
d. Plants that can live in very wet climates

6. Instead of grass, what did Mrs. Juarez put on her lawn to keep dust and dirt from blowing around?

a. Lavender
b. Yucca
c. Aloe
d. Gravel

7. What did Barry mean when he said, "You just moved in. Shouldn't we give presents to you?"

a. Mrs. Juarez was too busy to give presents
b. Traditionally, new neighbors receive gifts, not give them
c. Mrs. Juarez doesn't know Barry and Manolo well enough to know what they want
d. Barry and Manolo shouldn't take gifts from strangers

8. In paragraph 3, what does the word "knit" mean?

a. Join together tightly
b. Make clothing
c. Grow grass
d. Make nets

Questions 9–11 pertain to the following letter:

Thomas's First Complaint Letter

February 24, 2011

Thomas Goodwill

1234 Main Street

Thompson, Texas 77482

Romco Toys

8765 Madison Avenue

New York, New York 10008

To the customer service department:

I bought a Romco talking wind-up doll for my little sister from your website on November 12, 2010. The doll arrived on November 20. My sister opened the box on Christmas Day, and the doll worked fine until three days ago. At that time, my sister noticed that the winding part was getting harder to twist. Now it will not twist at all. The doll no longer talks.

My mom noticed that the papers that came with the doll state that it is guaranteed to work for one year. The papers also state that if the doll stopped working within a year, we should send it back to your company for a replacement. The doll is enclosed in this box. We would like a new doll to replace this defective one.

Thank you for your time. My sister looks forward to getting a new doll that works.

Sincerely,

Thomas Goodwill

9. Why did Thomas write this letter?

a. To invite a friend over for Christmas
b. To replace a doll he bought that broke
c. To buy a wind-up talking doll
d. To ask about a wind-up talking doll

10. How long is the guarantee for the doll?

a. One year
b. One month
c. Two years
d. Three months

11. What does the word "defective" mean?

a. Ugly
b. Definitive
c. Broken
d. Expensive

Questions 12–18 pertain to the following letter:

Romco's Toys Reply Letter

March 5, 2011

Customer Service Department

Romco Toys

8765 Madison Avenue

New York, New York 10008

Dear Customer:

Romco's wind-up doll was a very popular item with girls this Christmas. Unfortunately, many of the toys sold before the holidays had a defective winding mechanism that gradually became harder to turn. It made it impossible to operate the doll's unique speaking features. This defect is the responsibility of the manufacturers, so we are asking our customers to help the company recoup some of the loss it experienced due to this problem.

Included in this letter is a form we are asking all customers to fill out to receive a replacement doll. The form provides Romco with the documentation necessary to recover money lost from replacing the defective dolls. Please fill out the form and put it in the prepaid envelope provided. Romco will assume all postage costs for the letter and the replacement doll. After the form is received, Romco will send a new doll free of charge. Thank you for your concern in this matter.

Sincerely,

Romco Customer Service Department

12. What did Romco Toys agree to do for Thomas?

a. Fix the old doll and return it
b. Give Thomas a coupon to buy a new doll
c. Talk to the manufacturer about the problem
d. Send Thomas a replacement doll

13. What did Romco Toys ask Thomas to do?

a. Operate the doll's unique speaking features
b. Fill out a form and send it to Romco Toys
c. Write to the manufacturers about the problem
d. Buy a new doll

14. The following are five statements about the Romco doll. Which of these statements is an opinion about the doll? Select all that apply.

a. Thomas purchased the doll on November 12, 2011
b. The doll worked on Christmas Day
c. The doll had a pretty voice
d. The doll stopped working in February
e. The doll was cheaply made

Questions 17-21 pertain to both Thomas's letter and Romco Toy's reply letter:

15. According to both letters, what is the correct format for writing the name of a town and state in an address?

a. Anywhere. Texas
b. Anywhere: Texas
c. Anywhere Texas
d. Anywhere, Texas

16. Why did Romco Toys call Thomas "Customer" in its letter?

a. Romco Toys had so many complaints it couldn't write individual letters.
b. Thomas did not write his name in his letter.
c. In the letter, Romco Toys said it is standard procedure to not use customers' names.
d. Thomas was not a customer; his sister received the doll.

17. How long did it take Romco Toys to reply to Thomas's letter?

a. Two weeks
b. Two months
c. Nine weeks
d. Nine days

18. Tone in writing describes the feelings or impressions a piece of writing give the reader. Just a few examples of tone are happy, sad, polite, and angry. Which of the following best describes the tone of both letters?

a. Angry
b. Polite
c. Silly
d. Rude

Questions 19–28 pertain to the following passage:

Hobie's Journey across the Finish Line

(1) "On your marks, get set, GO!"

(2) While the crack of the starting gun was still ringing in his ears, Hobie straightened his right leg so fast he felt a twinge in his knee. He then swung his left leg straight in front of him. When he looked up, he was surprised to find himself nearly halfway up the track. His heart was thumping hard and fast in his chest.

(3) "Go easy," Hobie thought. "You have three-and-a-half more laps to go."

(4) He took a deep breath and lifted his legs slightly to relax his stride. His shoulders dropped a little as he swung his arms. Hobie's chest felt a little less tight. His feet tapped the track as Hobie matched the sound of his footfalls to those of the runners behind him.

(5) "Try to save some steam for the end," said Coach Bennett. "That's when you can catch up to the jack rabbits that used up everything in the first lap."
3. Hobie loved going fast for as long as he could remember. In kindergarten, he was always first to cross the finish line during running races at recess. He won an award in second grade for running the fastest mile in gym. But every spring, Hobie chose playing baseball over track, despite his parent's pleas to consider track.

(6) "You're such a good runner," said his mother. "And it would be so much easier because we would only have to drive to one practice."

(7) Hobie's older brother, Martin, was a member of the county's local track club. Martin had joined seven years earlier and was now one of the team's star sprinters. But Hobie did not want to be compared to his brother on the track. Few people in the town's Little League association even knew that Hobie had a brother, much less a brother who could run 100 meters in less than 15 seconds. Hobie wasn't the strongest player on his baseball team. He didn't like spending so much time on the bench, but he loved how he was always called "Hobie" or "Hobie Smith," never "Martin's little brother."

(8) Three months ago, in March, Hobie was all set for his fifth year in Little League. He had been practicing throwing and batting after school. His aim was improving, and so was his throwing speed. Hobie hoped his efforts would mean he would spend more time in his position, right outfield, and less time on the bench. Then Hobie and

Martin's father had an accident at work. Mr. Smith fell from a ladder and broke his leg and arm. He could not work or drive for six months.

(9) "I don't have time to get home from work and drive to two different practices," said Hobie's mother, Mrs. Smith, to Hobie. "And it's not fair to make Martin switch to baseball after he's been in track for seven years and is doing so well. I'm sorry Hobie, but you have only one choice for a sport this spring, and it's track. You don't have to join, but if you don't, you're staying home with Dad."

(10) Luckily, the coach for Hobie's track team, Coach Bennett, was new. He didn't know Hobie even had a brother. Also, Hobie turned out to be better at long distances. Coach Bennett had him focus on the mile and the 800-meters events. At the last meet, Hobie ran a mile in just under seven minutes.

(11) "You keep that up, and I'm kidnapping you for the high school cross-country running team in the fall!" Coach Bennett joked after the race.

(12) Hobie was now finishing his first turn with only two other runners ahead of him. He couldn't believe how well he had done this season. In baseball, Hobie always struggled to pay attention in the field. He loved batting, running bases, and catching fly balls, but hated the endless hours of waiting out in the field or on the bench for something to happen. In track, he was always moving. And, for the first time, he was doing very well. He was the fastest distance runner on his team, and had won three out of the seven races he ran that season. Hobie pushed his legs a bit faster and caught up to the second-place runner. There was just one person blocking his view of the finish line.

(13) Hobie felt his legs fly through the air and his chest start to hurt a little. He puffed his cheeks and swung his arms hard. Two more laps to go. Hobie kept pace a few feet behind the runner in the lead until they rounded the last bend of the track. Hobie drew a deep, ragged breath and started to run a little faster, making the distance between him and the other runner a few feet shorter. Hobie kept sprinting until he was running side by side with the runner in the lead. The finish line came into view. With his last ounce of strength, Hobie pushed past the other runner and swung his arms as hard as he could, flying over the finish line four yards ahead of the other runner.

(14) "Good job!" shouted Coach Bennett, rushing out to jog alongside him. Hobie slowed down and leaned over to catch his breath, placing his hands on his knees. Then he looked up into the stands and saw his father waving his good arm. Hobie waved back. He was no longer angry that he couldn't play baseball. He was glad to be running track.

19. Why did Hobie choose baseball instead of track?

a. Hobie's parents wanted him to play baseball
b. Hobie wanted to avoid being compared to his older brother
c. Hobie was a better baseball player than runner
d. Hobie's brother, Martin, also played baseball

20. In paragraph 2, what does the word "twinge" mean?

a. Hurt
b. Bend
c. Break
d. Loosen

21. Which sentence from paragraphs 5-7 shows that Hobie is a good runner?

a. "Hobie wasn't the strongest player on his baseball team"
b. "Hobie loved going fast for as long as he could remember"
c. "But Hobie did not want to be compared to his brother on the track"
d. "In kindergarten, he was always first to cross the finish line during running races at recess"

22. Which of the following phrases belongs in the blank in the Venn diagram below?

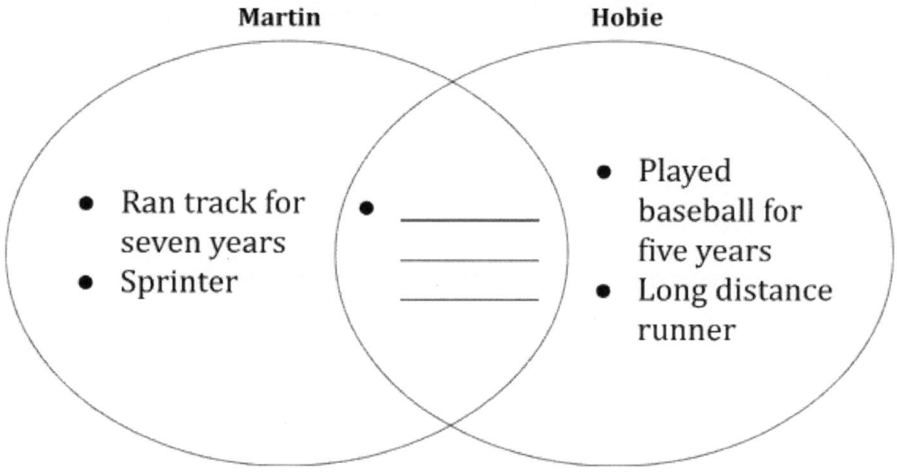

a. Good at running
b. Older brother
c. Younger brother
d. Ran on high school cross-country team

23. What is the most likely lesson a reader will learn from this story?

a. Track is a better sport than baseball
b. It is dangerous to use ladders
c. Hard decisions can have positive outcomes
d. Big brothers like to be compared to little brothers

24. Increased tension or excitement in a story is called suspense. How does the author build suspense in the story "Hobie's Journey across the Finish Line"?

a. By describing how Hobie's father hurt himself at work
b. By describing how Hobie got better at running long distances
c. By showing why Hobie had to switch to track from baseball
d. By describing how Hobie got from third to first place in the race

25. Which choice best summarizes the story?

a. Although Hobie did not like to run, his parents forced him to participate in track. Throughout the season, he never improved, and he lagged behind all of the other runners. In the final race, he came in last place. This only reaffirmed his belief that he was meant to play baseball instead.
b. Despite showing a talent for running, Hobie chose to play baseball to avoid comparisons to his older brother. His father's accident forced him to join track, where he did well, and his attitude towards track shifted.
c. Hobie was a naturally gifted sprinter. He won almost every race without having to practice. During his final race of the season, he left all his competitors far behind him which made for an easy victory.
d. Despite his talent in running, Hobie resented track and constantly compared himself to his brother, Martin. He was also a very good baseball player, but his parents made him join the same sport as his brother to make things easier after his father's accident.

26. What is the best definition of the word "ragged" as it is used in paragraph 13?

a. Roughly kept
b. Having a torn edge or outline
c. Worn-out from stress and strain
d. Wearing tattered clothes

27. Based on the events of this story, what is Hobie most likely to do next year?

a. Join track as a sprinter to compete against his brother
b. Join Little League and compete to be a pitcher
c. Join track as a long distance runner
d. Join Little League and play right field

28. Part A: As used in paragraph 1, what does the word "crack" describe?

a. A split in the track
b. The sound of the starting gun
c. The sound of a spectator clapping
d. A hurdle that was broken

Part B: Based on your answer in Part A which of the following is an appropriate synonym for "crack"?

a. break
b. fracture
c. split
d. snap

Questions 29–33 pertain to the following passage:

Sticky Water

(1) News flash: water is sticky. This is a surprise to many people because water does not seem sticky. In fact, it's the first thing that people reach for to wash away stickiness and any other kind of dirt. The second item, of course, is soap.

(2) Water and things like glue are sticky in different ways. Glue is sticky in two ways. Water is sticky in only one way. Glue feels and acts sticky. It is used to join objects such as paper, wood, and plastic together. Water does not feel or act sticky.

(3) Glue is sticky in two ways. One way is called adhesion. This is when glue, after it is poured on a surface, spreads into tiny holes and dents and hardens. The glue holds the surfaces together like the pieces of a jigsaw puzzle. But for glue to work well, it also needs to stick to itself and hold together. This is called cohesion.

(4) Water does not have adhesion. If you pour it on a piece of wood, the wood will absorb the water, but water will not harden to make two things stick together. Water does have cohesion. Water is a unique substance made up of two elements: hydrogen (H) and oxygen (O). Water is made up of two parts hydrogen and one part oxygen. The formula for water is H2O. The hydrogen atoms not only stick to the oxygen, but also to other water molecules, much in the same way magnets stick to metal. Water molecules stick to each other because of "hydrogen bonds." If water did not hold together, it could not be a liquid. It would boil and turn into steam.

(5) To see the "stickiness" of water, try the following experiment. This experiment is not dangerous, and it only requires ordinary objects that you probably have at home. However, you will end up spilling some water, so ask an adult if it is okay to do the experiment before starting.

Sticky Water Experiment

(6) You will need the following for this experiment:

- One short plastic cup (the kind adults use at parties for punch works very well)
- One small pitcher of water
- At least 20 pennies
- A sponge or rag for spills

(7) First, fill the plastic cup with water from the pitcher. Make sure you fill the cup all the way up to the rim. Don't spill any water! If you spill water, wipe it up. Make sure the very full glass is sitting on a dry spot.

(8) Next, carefully slip a penny into the cup and look closely. Did any of the water spill over the edge? Probably not. Continue adding pennies slowly to avoid splashing. Slip them in gently. Do not throw them in.

(9) Keep putting in pennies until water spills over the edge. How many pennies did it take for the water to spill over? It was probably more than you thought. Most people who do this experiment think one or two pennies will make the very full glass spill, but usually it takes more than 10 pennies. The explanation for this is cohesion. Each time you put in a penny, the water molecules hold on tighter and tighter to each other. Finally, when there is absolutely no more room in the glass

and they're hanging over the edge of the glass, the water spills. One time, a scientist was able to get 25 pennies into the glass before it spilled! Now that's sticky water!

29. Why did the author start this article with the words "News flash"?

a. To show it is a news article
b. The author made a mistake.
c. To attract readers' attention
d. Because it is a news story

30. Which of these phrases belongs in the blank line in the chart?

Different Kinds of Stickiness

Adhesion	Cohesion
• Sticks to surfaces • Fills in holes • Hardens • Acts like a jigsaw puzzle	• Sticks to other molecules in the liquid • Holds the liquid together • Does not harden • ______________________

a. Does not spill
b. Acts like a magnet on metal
c. Acts like water in a cup
d. Boils and turns into steam

31. Why is it important that the cup is sitting on a dry spot?

a. To keep adults from getting upset about the mess
b. To make the experiment safe and clean
c. To keep the pennies dry before they go in the water
d. To make it clear when the water spills from too many pennies

32. Why did the author call water sticky?

a. Because of the way the water molecules are attracted to each other
b. Because of the way water sticks to surfaces
c. Because of the way water feels on our hands
d. Because we use water to wash up sticky messes

33. Which of the following choices is the best example of how water is sticky?

a. The force of gravity makes rivers and streams flow downhill
b. Water combined with soap is useful for cleaning
c. A paper clip can float because of the surface tension of water
d. Too much water in a cup will spill over the edge

Questions 34–37 pertain to the following passage:

Water and Keeping It Clean

(1) We take water for granted. It is all around us in lakes, streams, pools, and oceans. We only need to turn on the tap to get some to drink or turn on the shower to wash ourselves with it. Water is everywhere. Most of the time we welcome having water, except when it floods into our basements or onto our floors.

(2) It's important to remember that water is a valuable and life-sustaining substance. Without water, humans and most animals and plants would die within a few days. Water is also unique. It is the only natural substance that can be in three states – liquid, solid (ice), and gas (steam). For water to change from one state to another, it has to change temperature. To stay in a liquid state, water must be between 33°F and 211°F. Water freezes, or turns into ice, at 32°F. It boils, or turns into steam, at 212°F.

(3) The freezing point for water does not change, but the boiling point for water changes depending on how high you are above sea level. The higher up you go, the lower the boiling point. So, water that will boil at 212°F by the ocean will only need to be 186.4°F to boil at 14,000 feet. That's good to know on your next hike up the Rocky Mountains!

(4) Here is another fun fact about water. When it is in its solid form, ice, it is less dense. Ice, which is strong enough to hold up a full-sized truck on a frozen lake, is lighter than water. That is why ice floats.

(5) Despite its unique qualities and its importance to our survival, water is almost constantly under attack, and the enemy is pollution. There are many things that pollute water, including chemicals in fertilizers that can be washed off fields and into streams when it rains. The waste we flush from our houses has pollutants. Most of it is treated at wastewater treatment plants, but a tiny amount still leaks back into lakes, rivers, and oceans.

(6) The good news is that many farmers are changing the way they take care of their crops to prevent chemicals from washing into rivers. Scientists and engineers are working with wastewater treatment plants to make them better at keeping all pollutants out of lakes and oceans.

(7) Even ordinary people can help keep water clean. Picking up trash helps keep it from blowing into nearby water sources. It is especially important to pick up plastic because plastic does not break down like paper and wood. Fish and other animals in the water get tangled in plastic bags. They may also mistake plastic objects for food, eat them, and die.

(8) So, next time you are out for a walk or at a park, be sure to pick up trash and make sure it ends up in a garbage can. You will not only make the place look better, but you will also be saving the lives of animals in the water and keeping the water clean.

34. What are the three states of water?

a. Solid, liquid, gas
b. Gas, steam, ice
c. Water, ice, solid
d. Liquid, solid, water

35. What is the boiling point of water at 14,000 feet above sea level?

a. 330.2°F
b. 211°F
c. 186.4°F
d. 212°F

36. Which of the statements about water are facts? Select all that apply.

a. There should be a stricter law against people who pollute the water.
b. Water pollution isn't the biggest problem facing the world today.
c. Fertilizers washed off of fields by rain pollute nearby streams, rivers, and lakes.
d. People who pollute the water are bad.
e. Water is the only natural substance that can be found in three states

37. Which of these is a "fun fact" that the article gives about water?

a. The waste we flush from our houses has pollutants.
b. The freezing point for water does not change, but the boiling point for water changes depending on how high you are above sea level.
c. When it is in its solid form, ice, it is less dense.
d. Water is also unique. It is the only natural substance that can be in three states – liquid, solid (ice), and gas (steam).

Questions 38–40 pertain to both articles "Sticky Water" and "Water and Keeping it Clean":

38. What is one idea expressed in both articles?

a. Water is a unique substance
b. All living creatures need water to survive
c. Water is wet
d. Water is sticky

39. How is the article "Sticky Water" different from "Water and Keeping It Clean"?

a. "Sticky Water" shows where water comes from and "Water and Keeping It Clean" talks about water pollution
b. "Sticky Water" mostly describes a property of water and "Water and Keeping It Clean" mostly talks about a problem related to water
c. "Sticky Water" is about cohesion and "Water and Keeping It Clean" is about adhesion
d. "Sticky Water" is a true story and "Water and Keeping It Clean" is made up

40. In what kind of book or magazine would these articles most likely be found?

a. English language arts
b. Social studies
c. Math
d. Science

Answers and Explanations for Reading Test #1

1. Part A: D: The main objective of these paragraphs is to describe Manolo's and Barry's neighborhood.

Part B: C: Since the main objective of the paragraphs is to describe the neighborhood, the sentence that talks about the lack of trees helps support the answer from above.

2. A: The strange thing about the name of Barry's and Manolo's neighborhood is that there are no Cypress trees and the land is flat.

3. A: The first sentence shows that Cypress Heights residents do everything in their control (painting their houses and decorating their lawns) to make their places look nice.

4. A: Barry and Manolo like living close to each other because it makes it convenient for them to visit each other.

5. C: Plants that can live in very dry climates are called drought-resistant.

6. D: Mrs. Juarez put gravel on her lawn instead of grass. She used gravel because she wouldn't have to water it.

7. B: Traditionally, new neighbors receive gifts, not give them. That is why Barry asked Mrs. Juarez that question.

8. A: Knit in this case means to join together tightly.

9. B: Thomas wanted to replace a doll he bought for his sister, which broke before the warranty was up.

10. A: The warranty or guarantee for the doll was for one year.

11. C: The word "defective" is another way of saying "broken."

12. D: The company agreed to send Thomas a replacement doll after he sent in some paperwork.

13. B: Romco asked Thomas to fill out a form and send it to them.

14. III & V: Remember that facts can be proven, but someone's opinion is debatable. Both of these statements can be debated.

15. D: The correct form for writing the name of a town and state is Anywhere, Texas.

16. A: Romco did not have time to write an individual letter to all of the customers with complaints, so they wrote a general letter to all people who complained.

17. D: It took nine days for Romco to reply to Thomas's letter according to the dates on the letters.

18. B: The tone in both letters is polite.

19. B: Hobie chose baseball because his brother was already running track and he didn't want to be compared to him.

20. A: Twinge also means to hurt. Hobie flexed his leg so fast that it made his knee hurt a little.

21. D: Always being the first one to cross the finish line is a good indication that Hobie was (and still is) a good runner.

22. A: While Martin and Hobie may be different in many ways, they are both good at running.

23. C: Hobie had a hard decision to make. Forced to give up baseball, he had to choose between playing a sport where he might be compared to his brother or staying at home. Hobie found out that difficult decisions sometimes turn out all right in the end.

24. D: The author's step-by-step account of how Hobie made it from third to first place in the race increased the tension or suspense in the story.

25. B: A summary is a brief overview of what happened and occurred in the story. This is the only option that correctly reflects the story. Answer choice D is most similar; however, Hobie was not a good baseball player. He simply preferred the sport over track because he wasn't compared to his older brother while he played.

26. C: Hobie's breathing became ragged because he was worn out from running so fast for so long.

27. C: Hobie is most likely to rejoin track the following year as a long-distance runner, an area where he showed talent. It will also allow him to avoid comparisons to his brother, who is a sprinter.

28. Part A: B: In the story it says, "While the crack of the starting gun was still ringing in his ears," which lets you know that it was the sound of the gun.

Part B: Knowing that is was the sound of the gun the only answer that makes sense is "snap".

29. C: The author started the story with the phrase "News flash" to attract the readers' attention. The article is about a scientific fact. It is not a breaking news story.

30. B: Cohesion is a kind of stickiness in which molecules stick to each other via attraction, much in the same way a magnet sticks to metal.

31. D: The point of the experiment is to see how many pennies it takes for an already full glass of water to overflow. That is why the glass must be in a clean, dry place.

32. A: Water is sticky because its molecules stick to each other.

33. C: A paper clip can float on top of water because the molecules are stuck together and can hold it up.

34. A: The three states of water are solid, liquid, and gas.

35. C: 186.4°F is the boiling point of water at 14,000 feet.

36. C, E: These sentences are both facts and can be proven. The other answer choices are all opinions.

37. C: In the article it states, "Here is another fun fact about water. When it is in its solid form, ice, it is less dense."

38. A: Both articles note that water is a unique substance.

39. B: The first article talks about a property of water (its stickiness) and the second article talks about a problem related to water (pollution).

40. D: Articles about the properties of water are most likely to be found in a science text.

Language Practice Test #1

Questions 1-4 pertain to the following passage:

Simon and His Father

(1) "Well, that about does it," said Simon, gluing the last decal on the rudder of his model B17G Flying Fortress plane.

(2) "We have to let the glue dry," said Pedro, looking down at the finished plane.

(3) "While we're waiting, let's go get your car," said Simon. (4) "It's only three o'clock, so the store is still open."

(5) "I'll go home and get my money," said Pedro, and then he left.

(6) Pedro was getting his money, Simon looked at his newly finished plane. (7) He and Pedro had spent about four hours building it. (8) It was the first time Simon had ever built a model airplane without his father's help. (9) His father had offered, but this time Simon said he wanted to try it on his own. (10) Pedro read the directions and handed Simon parts while Simon looked over Pedro's shoulder at the plans and carefully glued the pieces in place. (11) It was the hardest model Simon had ever built.

(12) Just then there was a knock on the door.

(13) "Can I come in?" asked Simon's father.

(14) "Sure," said Simon. (15) "Check out the plane!"

(16) "Wow," said Simon's father quietly, looking closely at the finished model. (17) "You and Pedro did a great job. (18) It looks just like the real thing."

(19) At that moment it occurred to Simon that his father, behind the proud smile, might feel hurt because Simon let Pedro help him after telling his father he wanted to build it alone. (20) "You're not mad?" Simon asked.

(21) "Mad?" asked Simon's father. (22) "About what?"

(23) "That I asked Pedro to help me after you offered," said Simon, taking his eyes from his father's face and looking at the model.

(24) "Simon," said his father, "of course I'm not mad. (25) I'm proud. (26) You and Pedro did a great job! (27) I think I can take some credit for teaching you, but this shows that you are ready to start tackling these kinds of projects on your own. (28) Or, of course, with a friend."

(29) "Thanks, Dad," said Simon, giving his father a hug. (30) "You did teach me a lot of things. (31) A few of them I remembered when the plane we were building. (32) Pedro knows a lot, too."

(33) "Speaking of Pedro, there's the doorbell," said Simon's father, giving Simon a quick last squeeze. (34) "Would you two like a ride to the store this time? (35) It is pretty heavy this time of day."

(36) "Yes, the traffic probably would be a lot worse now, so we could use a ride," said Simon. (37) "Thanks, Dad."

(38) "No problem," said Simon's father. (39) "I'll get the keys."

1. Which word would be the best to add to the beginning of sentence 6 to improve the transition?

a. Until
b. While
c. Because
d. Whether

2. Which of the following would be an effective supporting detail to add after sentence 9?

a. Simon did not think his dad could help him, so he asked Pedro to help because he had built more models.
b. Simon had been hoping to build the plane on his own, but Pedro was upset when he learned this.
c. But, when Pedro offered to stay and work with him, Simon decided that he could use Pedro's help.
d. However, Pedro said that Simon would need help, so Simon listened to Pedro and let him help instead.

3. Which of the following is the best revision of sentence 31?

a. A few of them, when we were building the plane, I remembered.
b. When the plane we were building I remembered a few of them.
c. I remembered a few of them when we were building the plane.
d. We were building the plane when I remembered a few of them.

4. Sentence 35 uses unclear wording. Choose the word that should be used instead of *it*.

_________ is pretty heavy this time of day.

Planes
Models
Money
Traffic

Questions 5-8 pertain to the following passage:

Creative Gardening

(1) With more and more cities appearing in America, having a backyard garden is getting more and more difficult. (2) Instead, those who want a garden are creating balcony gardens by squeezing a few plants, or even a dwarf fruit tree, into what small space they have available. (3) While many plants are adaptable to different locations, plants should be chosen based on the area the garden will be in.

(4) Sunlight is very important. (5) Plants need the Sun to perform photosynthesis. (6) However, some plants need more than others. (7) This means that a shady porch and a sunny balcony will be better for different plants. (8) An area that receives less than six hours of sunlight each day is considered "partial shade." (9) Vegetables, such as beets, carrots, and peas, and decorative plants, such as hostas, begonias, and violas, may thrive here. (10) Some plants do not do well at all in patio and balcony gardens. (11) Full-shade areas receive less than three hours of daily sunlight. (12) Some ferns and types of ivy suffer without much Sun. (13) However, gardeners have seen success with kale, broccoli, and radishes in shaded areas.

(14) Patio and balcony gardens also require different containers. (15) Planting directly in the soil is not possible. (16) This means that gardeners may have large pots, raised beds, hanging baskets, window boxes, or even rows of pots or boxes hung on the wall. (17) Depending on the amount of sun and wind, special soils or mulch may be needed to keep plants moist or to keep water from collecting. (18) These soils can be heavy, especially after watering, so gardeners should make sure that any balcony or railing can support the weight before placing pots or boxes. (19) Resin or plastic containers are lighter than ceramic or terra cotta pots. (20) Additionally, containers should be secured to keep them from being knocked down or blown by gusts.

(21) Some gardeners may prefer a practical vegetable garden or rows of herbs. (22) Others decorate their small garden spaces with a multitude of flowers that look and smell beautiful. (23) A gardener's personality can be seen in the type of garden he or she chooses to grow. (24) Whether a gardener wants to grow fruit, vegetables, flowers, or just be near shades of green, there are plenty of options. (25) In an area with enough sunlight, a bit of soil, and a few containers, a miniature paradise can be created.

5. Sentence 4 is not an effective topic sentence for paragraph 2. Which of the following sentences should be used in place of sentence 4?

a. The first thing to consider is sunlight.
b. Plants can grow well in different areas.
c. The Sun shines on gardens, balconies, and patios.
d. Photosynthesis depends on the Sun.

6. Which of the following is the best way to combine sentences 5 and 6?

a. Plants need the Sun to perform photosynthesis, however, some need more.
b. Plants need the Sun to perform photosynthesis, but some plants need more than others.
c. Plants need the Sun to perform photosynthesis, so some plants need more than others.
d. Plants need the Sun to perform photosynthesis; some need more though.

7. Which of the following sentences should be removed from paragraph 2?

a. Sentence 7
b. Sentence 9
c. Sentence 10
d. Sentence 13

8. Which of the following sentences should be added after sentence 25 to improve this essay's conclusion?

a. Gardeners must simply remember to consider the sunlight, soil, and space in which they plant their garden.
b. There are many different reasons to start a garden, as well as endless ways to create a successful one.
c. Different plants respond well to different conditions, so gardeners should carefully plan their gardens.
d. The only thing that limits an aspiring gardener with a small space is the extent of his or her imagination.

Questions 9-12 pertain to the following passage:

All About Worms

(1) Worms like night crawlers and earthworms help keep soil healthy by moving organic matter from the surface down into the soil. (2) Eventually, a tree leaf can take three to five years to decompose and be incorporated into the soil. (3) In forests infested with night crawlurs, this process can take as little as four weeks! (4) By speeding up the breakdown of plant material, earthworms also speed up the rate at which nutrients are precycled back to the plants.

(5) Worms and other soil organisms are a more necessary part of the soil food web. (6) Without them, all the organic matter would build up on the soil surface and never get down into the soil. (7) To grow healthy, productive plants, you need healthy, productive soil. (8) Organisms in the soil provide food for plants when they need it and in a form they can use.

9. Which change would correct the mistake in sentence 2?

a. Change *Eventually* to *Normally.*
b. Add a comma after *leaf.*
c. Change *to* to *too.*
d. Change *be* to *been.*

10. Which change would correct the mistake in sentence 3?

a. Change *In* to *On.*
b. Change *crawlurs* to *crawlers.*
c. Change *take* to *took.*
d. Change *four* to *for.*

11. Which word should be used in place of precycled in sentence 4?

By speeding up the breakdown of plant material, earthworms also speed up the rate at which nutrients are __________ back to the plants.

decycled
recycled
incycled
upcycled

12. Which change would correct the mistake in sentence 5?

a. Add a comma after *Worms.*
b. Change *are* to *is.*
c. Change *more necessary* to *necessary.*
d. No change is needed in sentence 5.

Questions 13-16 pertain to the following passage:

Hobie's Big Race

(1) Hobie felt his legs fly through the air and his chest started to hurt a little. (2) He puffed his cheeks and swung his arms hard. (3) Two more laps to go. (4) Hobie kept pace a few feet behind the runner in the lead until they rounded the last bend of the track. (5) Hobie drew a deep, ragged breath and started to run a little faster, making the distance between him and the other runner a few feet shorter. (6) Hobie kept sprinting until he was running side by side with the runner in the lead. (7) The finish line came into view, and he could hear his families cheering for him. (8) His older brother called out, Come on, Hobie! You can do it! (9) With his last ounce of strength, Hobie pushed past the other runner and swung his arms as hard as he could. (10) He flyed over the finish line four yards ahead of the other runner.

13. Which change would correct the mistake in sentence 1?

a. Change *his* to *him.*
b. Change *through* to *with.*
c. Add a comma after *air.*
d. Change *hurt* to *hert.*

14. Which change would correct the mistake in sentence 7?

a. Change *finish line* to *Finish Line.*
b. Change *came* to *comes.*
c. Change *hear* to *here.*
d. Change *families* to *family.*

15. Which change would correct the mistake in sentence 8?

a. Change *called* to *calling.*
b. Add quotation marks before *Come* and after *it!*
c. Change *Come* to *come.*
d. No change is needed in sentence 8.

16. Which change would correct the mistake in sentence 10?

a. Change *flyed* to *flew.*
b. Change *four* to *for.*
c. Add a comma after *yards.*
d. Change *the other runner* to *an other runner.*

Questions 17-19 pertain to the following passage:

Eye Color and How It Works

(1) One of a person's most unique characteristics is his or her eye color. (2) Eyes come in a variety of shades, and a person's eye color depends on the DNA of his or her parents. (3) Most children have the same eye color as one or both of their parents. (4) However, some children have a completely different hue.

(5) However, the shade of a person's eyes also depends largely on the concentration of melanin in his or her iris. (6) With pigment ranging from light blue to black, the iris shade is based on the amount of melanin a person has in their eyes. (7) The greater the concentration of melanin, the darker the eye color. (8) The most common eye color in the world, brown, is caused by high levels of melanin. (9) Melanin is produced in the body when a person is exposed to light. (10) Because of this, babies are often born with blue-gray eyes because they have very low melanin levels.

(11) All lighter eyes, such as blue and green eyes, have low concentrations of melanin. (12) However, genetics still play a role in causing a person's eye color. (13) Some eye colors, such as blue, are recessive traits. (14) Other colors, such as brown, are dominant traits that are more likely to be inherited. (15) However, eye color is determined by several genes. (16) This explains why children can have different eye colors than both parents and why siblings can have different ones.

(17) While 90% of the population of some European nations has blue eyes, this eye color appears in only 8% of the world's population. (18) The most common eye color, by far, is brown. (19) Early humans were most likely brown-eyed. (20) A genetic mutation, or an irregularity, is believed to have caused lighter eye colors.

(21) While blue eyes were already less common than brown, they are now even more rare. (22) As people with different eye colors continue to marry each other, the recessive blue eye color is decreasing. (23) Blue eyes can potentially see better at night. (24) Despite this, blue eyes are unlikely to completely disappear. (25) They will simply become less common.

(26) Other rare eye colors include green and hazel. (27) About 2% of all people have green eyes, and about 5% have hazel eyes. These eye colors come from different genes than blue and brown. (28) Green eyes are also a genetic mutation.

(29) However, green eyes have more melanin than blue eyes. (30) Hazel eyes have the most melanin aside from brown. (31) The back layer of a hazel-colored iris has the same amount of melanin as a brown eye, but the front layer, or stroma, has much less.

(32) Eye color is just one of the complex traits that a person can inherit. (33) While eye color patterns are shifting worldwide, each person's eye color remains a unique part of his or her identity and a sign of his or her genetics.

17. Which of the following sentences should be added before sentence 5 to create a better transition to the second paragraph?

a. Melanin can impact a person's eye color and determine their skin tone.
b. Genes determine many things about a person's appearance and health.
c. Though sunlight affects your melanin levels, sunlight can still harm your eyes.
d. Many people already know that eye color is determined by many different genes.

18. Which of the following sentences includes a supporting detail that should be added after sentence 13?

a. The amount of melanin a person has also depends on genes.
b. Having green-colored eyes is also a recessive trait.
c. This means that they are less likely to be inherited.
d. Multiple siblings can all inherit the same recessive trait.

19. The wording in sentence 16 is unclear. Choose the word that should replace *ones* in sentence 16.

This explains why children can have different eye colors than both parents and why siblings can have different __________.

melanin
genetics
eye colors
behaviors

Questions 20-23 pertain to the following passage:

Earthquakes in New Zealand

(1) Of the many interesting things about New Zealand, its geological activity is near the top of the list. (2) In New Zealand, you can encounter high mountains, active volcanoes, and many earthquakes. (3) This is because New Zealand lie on the boundary of the Australian and Pacific Plates. (4) These plates are pieces of the Earth's crust. (5) While the Pacific Plate lies under the Pacific Ocean the Australian Plate lies under Australia. (6) New Zealand's locashion on this boundary is responsible for its unique geological makeup.

(7) Upon visiting New Zealand, be prepared to experience an earthquake. (8) Earthquakes happen when there is a sudden burst of energy released at the Earth's crust, which is deep within the Earth. (9) This enurgy causes seismic waves to be sent off, which can cause the ground to shake and even crack. (10) The deeper the quake, the less damage will be seen on the surface. (11) The shallower the quake, the more surface damage is done.

20. Which change would correct the mistake in sentence 3?

a. Change *New Zealand* to *new Zealand.*
b. Change *lie* to *lies.*
c. Change *of* to *with.*
d. Add a comma after *Australian.*

21. Which change would correct the mistake in sentence 5?

a. Change *while* to *wile.*
b. Change *the Pacific Ocean* to *a Pacific Ocean.*
c. Add a comma after *Ocean.*
d. Change *lies* to *lied.*

22. Which change would correct the mistake in sentence 6?

a. Change *locashion* to *location.*
b. Change *is* to *are.*
c. Change *its* to *it's.*
d. No change is needed in sentence 6.

23 Which change would correct the mistake in sentence 9?

a. Change *enurgy* to *energy.*
b. Change *causes seismic* to *cause seismic.*
c. Change *can cause* to *did cause.*
d. Add a comma after *shake.*

Questions 24-28 pertain to the following passage:

Jack's First Christmas in Africa

(1) "Hi, Jack," said Mom. "How was your day?"

(2) "Fine, I guess," sighed ten-year-old Jack.

(3) "Is everything all right? You don't sound very convincing."

(4) "Yes, Mom, everything's fine."

(5) Really, though, Jack wasn't fine. He was homesick. He and his parents had moved to Africa six months earlier to be missionaries. Africa was very different than America, but most of the time Jack was happy. He had made friends at the school, he was getting used to the bizarre food, and even living in a hut had become enjoyable. But now it was close to Christmas, and Jack missed America more than ever.

(6) Some of the African people didn't even celebrate Christmas, and the ones who did had very different traditions. There were no authentic Christmas trees, no ornaments, and definitely no snow. He wouldn't be enjoying any of his mom's special Christmas cookies because there was no way to get the ingredients needed to bake them. And just what kind of present did Jack expect to get? No new video games, no new skateboard, no new toys at all. None of these things were available in the little village in the middle of the African jungle.

(7) Then, one day at school, their class began talking about Christmas.

(8) "Tell us, Jack. How do you celebrate Christmas in America?" said Wahid.

(9) "Well, first we put up a Christmas tree in our home."

(10) "A Christmas tree?" asked Jalil. "I have never heard of such a thing."

(11) "It's an evergreen tree, one that never loses its leaves. We hang all sorts of decorations all over it, even lights," said Jack.

(12) Jack's classmates listened in amazement to all that Jack had to share about Christmas in America. He told them about all the great food they ate and wrapping presents for his parents in beautiful red, green, silver, and gold paper. He told them about all the family get-togethers, the caroling on the cold winter nights, and the stockings filled with candy and all kinds of treats. He even told them about the special candlelight service they always attended on Christmas Eve.

(13) "Christmas is really about giving, and spending time with friends and family," said Jack.

(14) Finally, a week later, it was the last day of school before the Christmas holidays would start. Jack moved extra slow when he awoke, wishing more than ever he could just stay in his bed. He didn't want to celebrate Christmas in Africa. It just wasn't the same. He dreaded going to school, but he knew he had no choice.

(15) When Jack walked into his classroom, he couldn't believe his eyes. There before him was a Christmas tree! It wasn't the kind of tree he had in America, but it was a tree, and it was covered in decorations, homemade versions of the ones Jack had described to his class. There were presents under the tree, wrapped in paper that had been painted. The colors were red and green with accents of gold and silver. On the table, there were several dozen special African cookies, along with some punch.

The students had even cut up tiny pieces of paper and strewn them all over the floor to look like snow.

(16) "Surprise, Jack!" said Wahid. "We wanted to bring American Christmas to you here in Africa."

(17) "Yes," said Jalil. "We know you miss your home, but we are glad you are here to celebrate Christmas with us this year."

(18) "Open your present, Jack," said Ourja.

(19) Jack tore the paper off the present and found a mitt and ball for playing a native African stick game.

(20) Jack smiled. "Thanks, guys," said Jack. "It looks like it's going to be a merry Christmas after all!"

24. What type of sentence is the sentence below?

"There were no authentic Christmas trees, no ornaments, and definitely no snow."

a. Simple
b. Compound
c. Complex
d. Compound-complex

25. Which change should be made to the sentence below?

"Jack moved extra slow when he awoke, wishing more than ever he could just stay in his bed."

a. change *extra slow* to *extra slowly*
b. change *extra slow* to *very slow*
c. change *extra slow* to *extremely slower*
d. change *extra slow* to *extra slowest*

26. What is the best way to combine these two sentences?

"Really, though, Jack wasn't fine. He was homesick."

a. Really, though, Jack wasn't fine, he was homesick.
b. Really, though, Jack wasn't fine because he was homesick.
c. Really, though, Jack wasn't fine, and he was homesick.
d. Really, though, Jack wasn't fine, but he was homesick.

27. What is an alternative word for "strewn" in the sentence below? Select all that apply.

"The students had even cut up tiny pieces of paper and strewn them all over the floor to look like snow."

a. dispersed
b. stacked
c. tossed
d. scattered
e. piled

28. The passage is "Jack's First Christmas in Africa" is best described as what type of text?

a. Narrative
b. Expository
c. Persuasive
d. Instructional

Answers and Explanations for Language Test #1

1. B: Sentence 6 describes what Simon did during the time Pedro was gone. Pedro got his money at the same time that Simon was looking at the plane. The transition at the beginning of sentence 6 should show this relationship. Choice B is correct because it means that the events were happening at the same time. Choice A is incorrect because it would mean that Simon looked at the plane until Pedro left to get his money. This is not true because Simon looked at the plane after Pedro left. Choice C is incorrect because it would mean that Pedro getting his money is the reason that Simon began looking at the plane. The passage does not support this idea. Choice D is incorrect because it suggests that it is unclear whether or not Pedro was getting his money. The passage confirms that he was, so *whether* is not a good choice for this sentence.

2. C: Choice C shows why Pedro was helping Simon after Simon told his father that he did not want help. The sentence in choice C shows that Simon changed his mind and realized that Pedro's help would be a good thing to have. Choice A is incorrect because Simon's father is the one that taught him how to build models. Simon knows that his father can help him. Choice B is incorrect because Simon later states in sentence 23 that he asked Pedro to help him. Additionally, the story does not show that Pedro had gotten upset. Choice D is incorrect because Simon has built models before and knows how difficult it can be. The story does not support the idea that Simon would listen to Pedro over his father.

3. C: Sentence 31 does not present information in a logical order. Choice C clearly states the information in an order that makes sense and is easy to read. Choices A and B are incorrect because they are not clear or easy to understand. Choice D is incorrect because it changes the meaning of the sentence. Choice C suggests that Simon remembered his father's teaching as he and Pedro built the plane, and that it helped him. However, choice D suggests that Simon and Pedro had already made progress on the plane before Simon remembered what his father had taught him. It also does not present information in the most logical order.

4. Traffic: In sentence 34, Simon's father offers to drive the boys to the store. In sentence 36, Simon confirms what his father said in sentence 35 by saying that traffic has probably gotten worse. This shows that Simon's father is talking about traffic in sentence 35. The other answers are not logical. Simon's father says "It is pretty heavy this time of day," so the time affects how heavy the subject is. Planes, models, and money do not become heavier with time. The time does not change their weight or make more of them appear, so these answer choices are incorrect.

5. A: Sentence 4 is not effective because it does not give the reader any information or show what the topic of the paragraph is. The purpose of paragraph 2 is to tell gardeners that they should consider the amount of sunlight that plants need. Choice A states this and gives the reader a better idea of the topic of the paragraph. Choice A is correct. Choice B is incorrect because this information has already been given in sentence 3. This sentence also does not tell the reader what the paragraph is about. Choice C is incorrect because it does not provide needed information. The reader knows that the Sun can shine in different places. This sentence also does not connect sunlight to gardening, it simply states that the Sun shines on gardens. Choice A, however, shows that gardeners need to think about sunlight when planning their gardens. Choice D is incorrect because this information is stated in sentence 5 and does not show the topic of the paragraph.

6. B: The new sentence should include the information given in lines 5 and 6. This sentence includes the fact that plants need the Sun for photosynthesis and the fact that not all plants need the same amount of sunlight. The sentence should also be complete, grammatically correct, and clear. The only answer choice that correctly does this is choice B. Answer choice A incorrectly adds a comma before the word "however," and it is not super clear. Answer choice C uses the conjunction "so" which does not make sense when combining these two sentences. Answer choice D is abrupt and unclear.

7. C: Sentence 10 should be removed because it does not support the paragraph and is not needed. Paragraph 2 is about the amount of sunlight that different plants need. Sentence 10 simply states that some plants cannot live in patio and balcony gardens. This does not help the reader understand the topic of the paragraph or the other information given, so choice C is correct. Choice A is incorrect because this sentence gives examples of different areas with different sunlight and supports the information in sentences 5 and 6. Choice B is incorrect because sentence 9 gives examples of plants that can live in partial shade. This supports the information in sentence 8. Choice D is incorrect because it provides information that supports the paragraph and helps the reader understand the information that is given.

8. D: The concluding sentence should be related to the overall topic of the passage. It should also give the reader a sense that the passage has reached its end. The concluding sentence should not focus on one small detail or state any information that was not given somewhere else in the passage. Choice D is the best choice because it relates to the overall topic of the passage, which is gardening with a small space. It also summarizes the ideas in the passage by suggesting that there are many ways to create a garden in a small space. Choice A is incorrect because it does not relate to the topic of small gardens. It also simply restates the topic of each body paragraph. Choice B is incorrect because it is not related to the topic of the passage. Choice C is incorrect because it focuses on small details instead of the overall topic.

9. A: The word *eventually* does not fit at the beginning of this sentence. Sentence 2 is describing how long most tree leaves take to decompose. Since this sentence is not describing one event, *eventually* should not be used here. *Normally* should be used, since it shows that the sentence is talking about a process that happens often and can happen differently. Choice A is correct. There is no need to add a comma after *leaf*, so choice B is incorrect. The word *to* is a preposition, and the word *too* is a synonym of *also*. In sentence 2, the word *to* is used as a preposition, so it is spelled correctly, and choice C is incorrect. *Be* is a present-tense verb, and *been* is a past-tense verb. Sentence 2 is in the present tense, so it should use present-tense verbs. *Be* is used correctly in sentence 2, so choice D is incorrect.

10. B: The word *crawlers* is spelled using the suffixes *-er* and *-s*. In sentence 3, it is misspelled as *crawlurs*, so choice B is correct. The process of leaves decaying takes place within a forest, not on top of or over the forest, so choice A is incorrect. *Take* is a present-tense verb, and *took* is a past-tense verb. Sentence 3 is in present tense, so the verb *take* is used correctly and choice C is incorrect. The word *four* is a number and the word *for* is a preposition. In sentence 3, the word *four* is used to show how many weeks it may take for a leaf to decay. *Four* is spelled correctly, so choice D is incorrect.

11. recycled: The prefix *pre-* means something happens before something else. The prefix *re-* means that something happens again. This sentence says that the nutrients are going through a process that puts them into plants again. This shows that the word that goes in the blank should show something happening again. Since the prefix *re-* means "happening again," *recycled* is the correct word. *De-* means that something is removed or undone. *In-* means that one thing is within another, or that one thing is the opposite of another. The word *upcycled* means that parts of objects are put together to create something new. *Incycled*, *decycled*, and *upcycled* do not fit the meaning of this sentence, so they are all incorrect.

12. C: Comparative adjectives are used when comparing two things, and they usually end in the suffix *-er* or are used with the word *more*. Standard adjectives are used to describe just one thing. In this sentence, the word *necessary* is used to describe one group of organisms. As written, it is used with the word *more*, so it is used as a comparative adjective. Since *necessary* only describes one thing, it should be a standard adjective. *More* should be removed from the sentence, so choice C is correct. *Worms* is an item in a list of only two items, so no comma is needed and choice A is incorrect. *Are* is a plural verb, and *is* is a singular verb. The word *are* follows the noun *organisms*, which is plural. Since *organisms* is plural, it should be used with a plural verb like *are*, so choice B is incorrect. Choice D is incorrect since *more* needs to be removed from the sentence.

13. C: Sentence 1 is written using two independent clauses. Independent clauses should be joined by either a semicolon or a comma followed by a coordinating conjunction. Sentence 1 includes two independent clauses and a coordinating conjunction, but no comma. A comma should be added after *air*, so choice C is correct. *His* is a possessive pronoun, and *him* is an objective pronoun. *His* is used in sentence 1 to show that the sentence is talking about the legs and chest belonging to Hobie. A possessive pronoun is the correct type of pronoun to use in sentence 1, so choice A is incorrect. Sentence 1 says "Hobie felt his legs fly through the air." The preposition *with* is used to show that two nouns are completing an action together or that two events are happening at the same time. Hobie's legs are flying, but the air is not flying with them. *Through* is the right preposition to use in this clause, so choice B is incorrect. *Hurt* is spelled with a *u*, not an *e*, so choice D is incorrect.

14. D: The word *family* is a collective noun that is used instead of naming the members of the family. Even though *family* represents multiple people, it is a singular noun. *Families* is the plural form of *family*. Only one family is mentioned in sentence 7, so choice D is correct. The finish line in this story is not a proper noun, so choice A is incorrect. Sentence 7 is written in the past tense. *Came* is a past-tense verb, and *comes* is a present-tense verb. *Came* is used correctly in sentence 7, so choice B is incorrect. *Hear* means that someone can detect a sound. *Here* is used instead of naming a specific place. In sentence 7, Hobie can detect the sound of his family cheering for him, so *hear* is the correct word to use. Choice C is incorrect.

15. B: Dialogue, or words spoken by a character, should include quotation marks. The quotation marks should be placed before the first word in the dialogue and after the last word in the dialogue. Hobie's brother's dialogue begins with *Come* and ends with *it!*, so choice B is correct. *Called* is a past-tense verb, and *calling* is a present-tense verb. Since sentence 8 is written in the past tense, *called* is used correctly, and choice A is incorrect. When dialogue starts with a new sentence, the first word in the dialogue should be capitalized. Hobie's brother's dialogue begins with a new sentence, so the first word, *come*, should be capitalized. Choice C is incorrect. Since quotation marks needed to be added to the sentence, choice D is incorrect.

16. A: *Fly* is an irregular verb because when it is written in past tense, it is not spelled by adding *-ed* to the present-tense form of the verb. In past tense, *fly* becomes *flew*, so choice A is correct. *Four* is a number, and *for* is a preposition. Sentence 10 describes how many yards were between Hobie and the runner behind him. This means that *four*, the number, is used correctly in this sentence, so choice B is incorrect. Commas do not usually need to be added before prepositional phrases, so choice C is incorrect. *The* is a definite article used to point out a specific thing. *An* is an indefinite article used to point out any one of something. The sentence is talking about one specific other runner, so *the* is the correct article to use, and choice D is incorrect.

17. D: Choice D is correct because it connects the information from paragraph 1 to the information from paragraph 2. It mentions genes and eye color, but it also suggests that there is more to know about eye color. The next sentence begins with *however*, which shows that the information in sentence 5 will contrast the information in the new sentence. Choice A is incorrect because contains the information given in sentence 5. Choice B is incorrect because it is about genes in general, not eye color. Choice C is incorrect because it tells the reader that sunlight impacts melanin and can harm a person's eyes. This sentence is not related to the information in the first paragraph. Additionally, the fact that sunlight can harm a person's eyes is off topic from the rest of the paragraph and the passage.

18. C: Sentence 13 says that some eye colors are recessive traits. A new sentence added after sentence 13 should help the reader understand what a recessive trait is. Choice C is correct because it helps the reader understand the meaning of "recessive trait." This definition is also supported by sentence 14. Sentence 14 says that a dominant trait is different from a recessive trait and is likely to be inherited. Choice A is incorrect because it does not support the information in sentence 13. Choice B is incorrect because it does not help the reader understand what a recessive trait is. It only gives another example, so it is repetitive and unnecessary. Choice D is incorrect because it also does not support the information in sentence 13 or help the reader learn what a recessive trait is.

19. eye colors: Sentence 16 says that children can have different eye colors than their parents. It then says that siblings can have a different quality from each other. The other sentences in the third paragraph are about how eye color is determined. These facts provide context that shows that siblings can have different eye colors, so "eye colors" is the correct answer. Since the rest of the paragraph is about how genetics affect eye color, it would not make sense to replace *ones* with *melanin*. While siblings can have different genetic traits, eye color is more specific than genetics, so *genetics* is not the correct answer. This passage is about physical traits, not behaviors, so *behaviors* is incorrect.

20. B: In the present tense, *lie* is a plural noun and *lies* is a singular noun. Since New Zealand is one country, it should be used with a singular noon. *Lie* should be changed to *lies*, so choice B is correct. *New Zealand* is the full name of a country, so it is a proper noun and both words should be capitalized. This makes choice A incorrect. Changing *of* to *with* in sentence 3 would change the meaning. This would suggest that New Zealand, the Australian Plate, and the Pacific Plate are all on top of the boundary. However, the boundary is created by the edges of the plates, so this is incorrect. Choice C is incorrect. *Australian* is an item in a list of only two items, so a comma is not needed after *Australian*. Choice D is incorrect.

21. C: The word *while* is used as a subordinating conjunction in this sentence. It is used at the beginning of a clause, which makes that clause dependent. When a dependent clause comes before an independent clause, a comma must be used after the dependent clause. The dependent clause ends with the word *Ocean*, so a comma should be added after *Ocean*, making choice C correct. The word *while* is spelled with an *h*, so choice A is incorrect. There is only one Pacific Ocean, so the definite article *the* should be used with it, making choice B incorrect. *Lies* is a present tense verb, and *lied* is a past tense verb. Since sentence 5 is in the present tense, it should contain present tense verbs. *Lies* is the correct verb to use in this sentence, so choice D is incorrect.

22. A: The word *location* is spelled using the word *locate* and the suffix *-ion.* The letters *tion* are often pronounced like *shun*. However, the correct spelling uses a *t*, so choice A is correct. *Is* is a singular verb, and *are* is a plural verb. *Location* is a singular noun, so its action should be described using a singular verb, like *is*. Choice B is incorrect. *Its* is a possessive pronoun used to show something that an object has. *It's* is a contraction for *it is*. The sentence is stating that New Zealand has unique geology, so *its* is the correct word to use, and choice C is incorrect. Choice D is incorrect because sentence 6 contains a spelling error.

23. A: The word *energy* is spelled using two *e*s, even though they are pronounced differently in the word. *Enurgy* is a misspelling, so choice A is correct. When used in the present tense without a helping verb, *causes* is a singular verb, and *cause* is a plural verb. In this sentence, *causes* is used without a helping verb to describe the action of energy, which is a singular noun. *Causes* is used correctly, so choice B is incorrect. Later, *cause* is used with a helping verb. The verb *can* is used to show that something may happen in the future, and the verb *did* is used to show that something happened in the past. Since this verb is describing what seismic waves may do, *can cause* is used correctly, and choice C is incorrect. *Shake* is one item in a list of two items, so it should not be followed by a comma. Therefore, choice D is incorrect.

24. A: The sentence has only one subject and one verb. Even though multiple items were listed, there was only a single independent clause and no dependent clauses.

25. A: Adjectives modify nouns and adverbs modify verbs. In the original sentence, "slow" is an adjective modifying the verb "moved." Therefore, it should be changed to the adverb "slowly." Answer choice B is incorrect since "slow" is still an adjective modifying a verb. Answer choice C uses the word "extremely" before a comparative adjective. Answer choice D uses the word "extra" before a superlative adjective.

26. B: Answer choice B logically connects the two ideas in a grammatically correct way. Answer choice A uses a comma splice. Answer choice C does not clearly show a cause-effect relationship between Jack not being fine and being homesick. Answer choice D suggests a contract when the reason Jack is not fine is because he is homesick.

27. A, C, D: Dispersed, tossed, and scattered are all synonyms for the word strewn. This means they were spread out throughout the room. Stacked and piled mean that it was grouped together in a singular location, so answer choices B and E could not be correct.

28. A: This story is a narrative since it tells a story with characters, dialogue, conflict, and resolution. It also has a beginning, middle, and end. It is not informational, and it does not provide procedural steps. It also is not trying to convince the reader of any point or belief.

Reading Practice Test #2

Questions 1–9 pertain to the following passage:

War: The Card Game

(1) Rain came down in sheets, drumming on the windows and then splashing on the tiny deck that stuck out from Mona and Yuri's third floor apartment. Mona looked out at the yard outside the apartment complex. Large puddles were forming in the middle of the lawn, making a small lake around a tree where she, her brother Yuri, and the neighborhood children liked to play.

(2) "I am so sick of this rain," said Mona. It was Saturday. Her mother, a nurse, was sleeping after working overnight at the hospital. Mona and her brother usually went outside to let her mother sleep, but the rain was so heavy that even with raincoats and hoods, they'd be drenched in minutes. They watched cartoons for a couple of hours, but soon grew restless. It was 11 a.m., too early to eat the lunch their mother had left them. It was also too early for their mother to wake up. She went to bed around 7 a.m. and didn't like to get up before 3 in the afternoon.

(3) "Let's play War," said Yuri.

(4) "War?" asked Mona. "Are you out of your mind? Mom is asleep. Running around the apartment and whooping it up will wake her in no time. You know how grumpy she gets when we wake her early."

(5) "This is a different kind of game," said Yuri. "My friend Peter taught it to me at the babysitter's yesterday afternoon. You play it with cards."

(6) "Cards?" said Mona. "How do you play War with cards?"

(7) "Like this," said Yuri. He took a deck of playing cards from the dining room cabinet. "First you shuffle them. I'm not very good at that."

(8) After Mona shuffled the cards Yuri dealt half the deck to Mona and half to himself. Then he put his cards face down in a pile in front of him and told Mona to do the same. He put his hand over the pile and told Mona to take the first card from the top of her pile and lay it down between them on the count of three.

(9)"One, two, three!" counted Mona and Yuri. Mona had a five and Yuri's card was a six.

(10) "The higher card wins, so I take this round," said Yuri, picking up both cards and setting them next to where he was sitting. Yuri explained that in the card game War, both players put down a card at the same time and the player with the higher valued card takes both cards. He explained that aces are the highest valued cards, followed by kings, queens, and jacks. Then the cards go by their numbers—10, 9, 8, and so on.

(11) "What if both players have the same number?" asked Mona.

(12) "That's when you have a war!" said Yuri excitedly. "If you both have the same number, you each put down two more cards face down and then turn the third card up. Whoever has the higher card then takes all eight cards. We play until we run out of cards and the player with the most cards wins. Isn't it easy?"

(13) "Yes," said Mona.

(14) Mona and Yuri continued playing until both of them put down a jack.

(15) "War!" they whispered excitedly.

(16) They put down two cards and then a third card that they placed face up. Mona had a queen and Yuri had a six. Mona took all eight cards. At the end of the game Mona had 30 cards and Yuri had 22.

(17) "I won!" said Mona excitedly.

(18) "Beginner's luck," said Yuri.

(19) "Actually, this game is all luck," said Mona.

(20) "True," said Yuri. "Want to go best out of three?"

(21) "You bet!" said Mona.

(22) They played for the rest of the morning, until it was time to eat lunch. In what seemed like no time at all, their mother was awake and they were planning a quick trip out of the house.

(23) "That was a great game," said Mona. "Thanks for teaching me, Yuri."

1. What does the writer mean by the phrase "rain came down in sheets"?

- **a.** It was raining on the laundry
- b. It was raining very hard
- c. It was raining lightly
- d. It was raining diagonally

2. Why couldn't Mona and Yuri run around the apartment and make noise?

- **a.** The downstairs neighbor would be angry
- b. There were strict rules against making noise before noon on weekends
- c. Mona was sick and couldn't stand loud noises
- d. Mona and Yuri's mother was asleep

3. What time was Yuri's and Mona's mother expected to wake up?

a. 7 a.m.
b. 11 a.m.
c. 3 p.m.
d. 5 p.m.

4. What kind of game did Yuri suggest playing?

a. A card game
b. A computer game
c. A board game
d. A running game

5. Which card has the highest value in War?

a. Ace
b. Queen
c. King
d. Jack

6. What has to happen in the game to have a "war"?

a. One player must have an ace.
b. Both players must have the same card.
c. Both players must run out of cards.
d. One player must have a king.

7. Who won the first game?

a. Yuri
b. Mona and Yuri's mother
c. Mona
d. Yuri and Mona tied.

8. What did Mona mean when she said "Actually, this game is all luck."?

a. The game does not require any skill to win
b. The game requires a lot of skill to win
c. Only lucky people win the game
d. A person needs lucky numbers to win

9. Mona and Yuri are playing War. Mona puts down a king and Yuri puts down a jack. Who wins the round?

a. Mona
b. Yuri
c. Nobody, because it's a tie
d. Nobody, because kings aren't allowed in the game

Questions 10–13 pertain to the following passage:

Ann Richards: The First Woman Governor of Texas

(1) Born Dorothy Ann Willis in 1933, Gov. Ann Richards did not start out in politics. She taught social studies and history at Fulmore Junior High School in Austin. Then, she got married and stopped teaching to raise her family. While at home, Gov. Richards volunteered for political campaigns and causes. She worked especially hard to make sure people were treated and paid fairly.

(2) In 1976, Gov. Richards successfully campaigned for the position of Travis County Commissioner. Six years later, she was elected Texas State Treasurer. She was the first woman in 50 years to be elected to a statewide office in Texas. She stayed in that office until 1990, when she was elected governor of Texas.

(3) As governor, Gov. Richards worked hard to make the state government work better. She asked that the records and budgets of every state agency be looked at carefully, a process called an audit. She changed the way decisions were made for schools by giving parents and teachers living and working in the district more power to make important decisions. She also worked to make Texas safer by opposing, or speaking out against, dangerous guns called assault weapons. She arranged for more education programs at prisons so that prisoners would have more chances to improve themselves.

(4) Gov. Richards appointed women and minorities to state government positions to increase opportunities within the state government for many different kinds of people. Gov. Richards served one term as governor. She lost in 1994 to George W. Bush, who later became president of the United States.

(5) Gov. Richards was famous for having a great sense of humor and not being afraid to make fun of herself. She once joked about her hair being heavily styled by saying, "Neither snow nor rain can move my hair." To show that women were just as capable as men, she once said about a famous dancing couple, "Ginger Rogers did everything that Fred Astaire did. She just did it backwards and in high heels." Gov. Richards kept working to make peoples' lives better, even after she left politics.

10. What did Ann Richards do before she entered politics?

a. Campaigned for the Travis County commissioner position
b. Became governor of Texas
c. Taught social studies and history
d. Audited Texas state agencies

11. Part A: What is paragraph 3 mostly about?

a. Gov. Richards's humor
b. Gov. Richards's life before politics
c. Gov. Richards's first job in politics
d. Gov. Richards's achievements as governor

Part B: Which sentence supports your answer?

a. She changed the way decisions were made for schools by giving parents and teachers living and working in the district more power to make important decisions.
b. Gov. Richards served one term as governor.
c. She stayed in that office until 1990, when she was elected governor of Texas.
d. To show that women were just as capable as men, she once said about a famous dancing couple, "Ginger Rogers did everything that Fred Astaire did. She just did it backwards and in high heels."

12. Which word below best describes "styled" as used in paragraph 1?

a. method
b. fixed
c. approach
d. grown

13. What did Richards mean when she said, "Neither snow nor rain will move my hair."?

a. Her hairstyle was very stiff and strong
b. Her hair was very important to her
c. She used to work in the post office
d. She needed strong hair to be governor of Texas

Questions 14–17 pertain to the following passage:

Kay Bailey Hutchinson: The First Woman Senator of Texas

(1) Kay Bailey Hutchinson was born and raised in Texas. She went to the University of Texas and graduated with a law degree in 1967. One of her first jobs was as a news reporter for a TV station. In 1972, Sen. Hutchinson ran for a seat in the Texas House of Representatives. In that job, Sen. Hutchinson worked with other representatives to make laws that would help people in Texas. She worked as a state representative for four years.

(2) Sen. Hutchinson is a hard working person who has constantly worked to improve her career. In 1976, she was given a chance to be the head of a board that worked to find safer ways to travel in the United States. She left Texas to work on the safety board, which was in Washington, D.C. In 1990, she was elected as the Texas State Treasurer, the same job that Gov. Richards had been elected to years earlier. As the state treasurer she cut the budget and fought against additional taxes. Then, in 1993, Sen. Hutchinson won a special election and was awarded one of two US Senate seats. In 1994, she won a full six-year term in the US Senate.

(3) Sen. Hutchison has worked hard as a senator. She worked to fix laws that changed the way money was spent for the military. She also wrote and helped pass a law that regulated shipping on the oceans. Sen. Hutchison also worked to give veterans and people who retired from the military health care benefits. In 2006, she was elected for a third time as a US Senator.

14. Part A: What kind of degree did Sen. Hutchinson get in 1967?

a. Master's degree
b. Doctoral degree
c. Law degree
d. Medical degree

Part B: What university did she receive it from?

a. Texas State University
b. Texas A&M University
c. Sam Houston State University
d. University of Texas

15. What did Sen. Hutchinson do for a job before she ran for a seat in the Texas House of Representatives in 1972?

a. Mother
b. TV news reporter
c. Lawyer
d. State treasurer

16. Part A: What is the main topic of paragraph 3?

a. Sen. Hutchinson's life before becoming a senator
b. Sen. Hutchinson's accomplishments as a state treasurer
c. Sen. Hutchinson's family
d. Sen. Hutchinson's accomplishments as a senator

Part B: Which two examples that support your answer in Part A.

a. "She worked to fix laws that changed the way money was spent for the military."
"Sen. Hutchison also worked to give veterans and people who retired from the military health care benefits."
b. "Sen. Hutchinson is a hard working person who has constantly worked to improve her career."
"In 1990, she was elected as the Texas State Treasurer, the same job that Gov. Richards had been elected to years earlier."
c. "Kay Bailey Hutchinson was born and raised in Texas."
"She also wrote and helped pass a law that regulated shipping on the oceans."
d. "In 1972, Sen. Hutchinson ran for a seat in the Texas House of Representatives."
"She worked as a state representative for four years."

17. What does "Sen." mean?

a. Senator
b. Sent
c. Sentry
d. Sensor

Questions 18-21 pertain to both passages: "Ann Richards: The First Woman Governor of Texas" and "Kay Bailey Hutchinson: The First Woman Senator of Texas":

18. Why are Gov. Richards and Sen. Hutchinson famous?

a. They were the first men to be governor and a US senator in Texas.
b. They were the first women to be governor and a US senator in Texas.
c. They were the first women to be teachers and news reporters in Texas.
d. They were the first women to have jobs outside of Texas.

19. What word belongs in the blank spot of the Venn diagram?

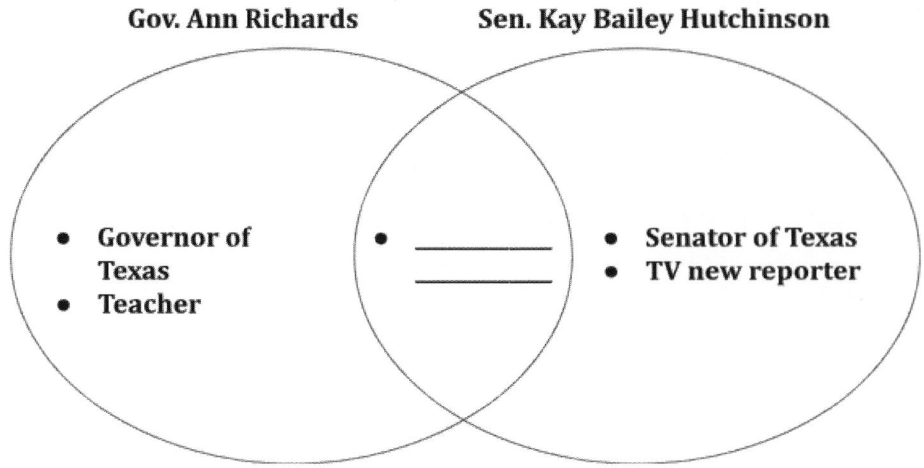

a. Senator
b. Governor
c. State treasurer
d. News reporter

20. Which woman is still working in government?

a. Ann Richards
b. Kay Bailey Hutchinson
c. Both
d. Neither

21. Why do you think the author wrote about these women?

a. To show that women can have the same opportunities as men in Texas
b. To explain the way government works in Texas
c. To show Gov. Richards's funny side
d. To show that men have the same opportunities as women in Texas

Questions 22–30 pertain to the following passage:

A Trip to Pavarti's House

Pavarti and Sam are in the same fifth-grade class at school. It is almost Halloween and Pavarti invited Sam to come to her house that weekend to carve pumpkins.

Pavarti (answering the phone): Hello?

Sam: Hello, is this Pavarti?

Pavarti: Yes, is this Sam?

Sam: Yes. Mom said I could come to your house tomorrow. She wanted to know what time would be good to drop me off.

Pavarti: We're going to buy the pumpkins in the morning and start carving after lunch. Why don't you come around 2 o'clock?

Sam: Sounds good. Mom wants to know how to get to your house. What is your address?

Pavarti: We live in town, at 145 State Street. Where do you live?

Sam: We're just outside of town on Route 20, at the intersection of Townline Road.

Pavarti: Take Townline Road north toward town. After two miles you will turn right on Elm Street.

Sam: Okay, I'm writing this down. Two miles, turn right on Elm Street.

Pavarti: Good. You will pass two traffic lights. At the third traffic light you will turn left to get on Rio Turnpike. Go about half a mile until you see a 7-Eleven on the right. The next street after the 7-Eleven is Main Street. Turn right onto Main Street.

Sam: Wait, wait, I want to make sure I get this right. Left on Rio Turnpike, at third traffic light. Go right at the 7-Eleven, half-mile down the road. It is Main Street.

Pavarti: That's right.

Sam: Where is your house after I turn onto Main Street?

Pavarti: We're all the way on the other end of the street. However, Main Street is one-way and you can't get to our house from the other end. Go past five streets. Our house is on the right side, in the middle of the sixth block.

Sam: (Writing it down) House is in the middle of the sixth block.

Pavarti: Yes. It is yellow and has a garage on the left. It is between a green house and a white house. It is the only yellow house on my block. Do not look for the address. It is very small and attached to the door in a crooked kind of way. It's really hard to see.

Sam: Okay, okay, let me write this down. Only yellow house on the block, between green and white houses.

Pavarti: Right. And there will be one or two cars in the driveway. Look for either a red truck or a small black car.

Sam: I have it all down. Our car is a white minivan. Hopefully you will not see it go by your house more than once!

Pavarti: (laughing) You should be fine. If you do get lost, just call us: 555-678-9101.

Sam: Sounds good. Hopefully we won't need it. Should I bring anything tomorrow?

Pavarti: Just your pumpkin carving skills. See you around 2 o'clock!

22. What is the main purpose of the telephone conversation?

a. To arrange a pumpkin shopping trip
b. To give Sam directions to Pavarti's house
c. To arrange a Halloween party at Sam's house
d. To give Pavarti directions to Sam's house

23. Pavarti is having Sam over. Why did Pavarti ask Sam where she lived?

a. So Pavarti could give Sam directions from her own house
b. So Pavarti could someday go to Sam's house
c. So Pavarti could find out whether Sam lives in town
d. So Pavarti could give directions to the closest 7-Eleven store

24. After Townline Road, what street does Sam's mother need to turn right onto?

a. Rio Turnpike
b. Main Street
c. Route 20
d. Elm Street

25. Why did Pavarti tell Sam the color of her house and the colors of the houses next to it instead of letting Sam use the address?

a. Because the address is hard to see from the road
b. Because Sam cannot read numbers
c. Because Pavarti does not know her address
d. Because the address is easy to see from the road

26. According to Pavarti, what direction should Sam's mother take if she enters at the bottom of the Rio Turnpike shown below?

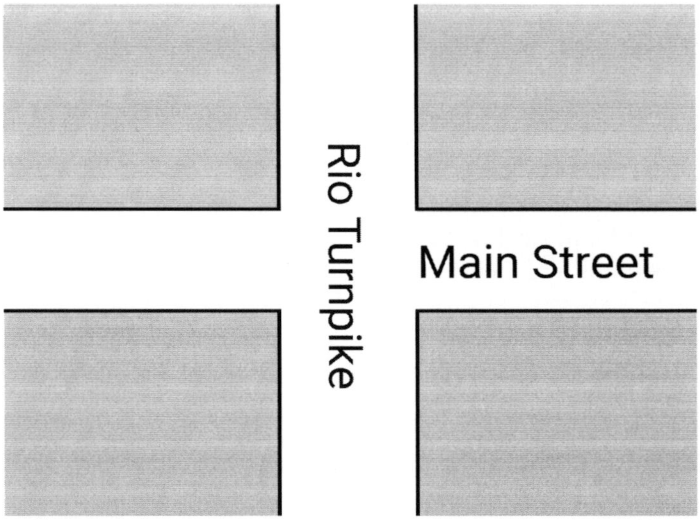

a. Straight, then right
b. Left, then straight
c. Straight, then left
d. Left, then right

27. Pavarti told Sam to look for a ______ truck or a ________ black car. Choose the answer that correctly fills in the blanks.

a. red, black
b. black, small
c. red, small
d. black, red

28. What did Sam mean when she said about her family's white minivan, "Hopefully you won't see it go by more than once!"?

a. Sam is hoping they don't drive the wrong way on Main Street
b. Sam is hoping they don't get lost and have to drive up and down Main Street
c. Sam is hoping Pavarti sees their car go by once
d. Sam is hoping the car doesn't break down

29. Sam wrote down the following notes while Pavarti was giving directions:

3 traf lghts. L on Rio Turnpk
7-Eleven on right, 1/2-mile down
Main Street

What part of Pavarti's directions did Sam write down?

a. Take Townline Road north towards town. After two miles you will turn right on Elm Street
b. It is yellow and has a garage on the left. It is between a green house and a white house. It is the only yellow house on my block
c. Main Street is one way and you can't get to our house from the other end. Go past five streets
d. At the third traffic light you will turn left onto Rio Turnpike. Go about half a mile until you see a 7-Eleven on the right. The next street after the 7-Eleven is Main Street

30. The following is Pavarti's morning schedule. What activity goes in the blank space?

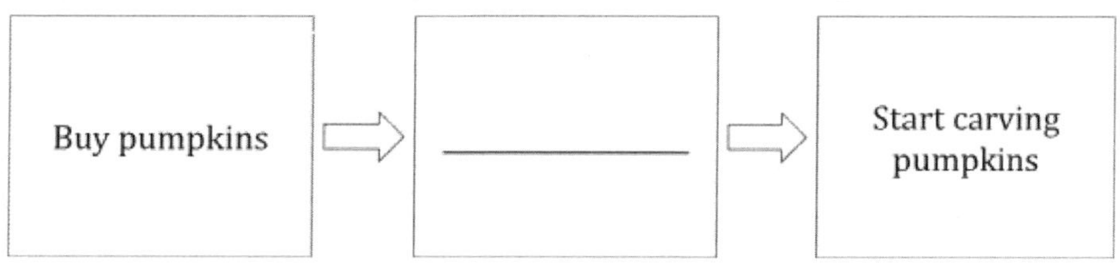

a. Take a nap
b. Pick up Sam
c. Give Sam directions
d. Have lunch

Questions 31–34 pertain to the following passage:

Simon and Pedro's Shopping Trip

(1) "Simon, where are you going?" asked Pedro. "You're missing your favorite show."

(2) Pedro had just arrived at Simon's house on his bicycle. He had ridden over to see what his best friend was doing on a Saturday morning at 10 o'clock. Simon was usually watching cartoons around this time.

(3)"I'm heading to the store," said Simon. "I've saved my allowance and I finally have enough money to buy the model plane I've wanted."

(4) "Great!" said Pedro. "Can I come with you? I want to see it. Also, can I help you build it when we get back?"

(5)"Sure," said Simon. "Let's go!"

(6) Simon and Pedro rode down the street and turned right onto the highway. The hobby store, which sold model planes, cars, and other model vehicles, was just a few hundred yards down the road. At the store Simon and Pedro took some time to look at the other models on the shelves.

(7) "Look!" said Pedro. "Here is a 1969 Mustang! It's $40! My dad said my grandfather used to own a real one. He bought it new and kept it for years. Then his brother, my uncle, bought it from him. Dad wishes he had never sold it."

(8) "Really?" said Simon. "I'd love to ride in one of those. Look at this! A C17! Man, I'd get this instead, but it's $50 and I only have $30."

(9) "What kind of plane were you planning to buy?" asked Pedro.

(10) "The model of that B17G Flying Fortress," said Simon. "I have just enough to buy it."

(11) "How much is it?" asked Pedro.

(12) "It costs about $25," said Simon. "But I also have to pay for the sales tax."

(13) "How much is tax?" asked Pedro.

(14) "Eight percent," said Simon. "My mom figured it out for me. It's $2. That leaves me with $3 change."

(15) "Do you get everything you need in the kit...like glue?" asked Pedro.

(16) "Good question," said Simon. "I'll ask."

(17) Simon went over to the clerk with the model airplane box in his hands. Pedro watched as the clerk nodded. He was hopeful that meant good news.

(18) "Yes," said Simon, walking back to Pedro. "Everything is included."

(19) "Well," said Pedro. "Let's head home and start building! When we're done, we'll break open my piggy bank and go buy the 1969 Mustang. Then we can play car chase."

(20) "Excellent!" said Simon, as he headed toward the counter with the box and his wallet.

31. Part A: What was the model that Pedro noticed in the store?

a. C17
b. B17G Flying Fortress
c. 1969 Mustang
d. A18H Flying Dutchman

Part B: Why did Pedro like that model so much?

a. It was the cheapest one
b. His grandfather had owned a real one
c. It was the easiest to build
d. His grandfather loved airplanes

32. What model did Simon want to buy, but couldn't afford?

a. C17
b. B17G Flying Fortress
c. 1969 Mustang
d. A18H Flying Dutchman

33. How much will Simon's model cost with tax?

a. $25
b. $27
c. $45
d. $50

34. What did Simon and Pedro plan to do after Simon bought his model?

a. Buy the 1969 Mustang too and build both of them together
b. Build the 1969 Mustang and then build the C17
c. Build the B17G Flying Fortress and then go buy the 1969 Mustang
d. Buy the 1969 Mustang and then build the B17G Flying Fortress

Questions 35–36 pertain to the following passage:

Simon and His Father

(1) "Well, that about does it," said Simon, gluing the last decal on the rudder of his model B17G Flying Fortress plane.

(2) "We have to let the glue dry," said Pedro, looking down at the finished plane.

(3) "While we're waiting, let's go get your car," said Simon. "It's only 3 o'clock, so the store is still open."

(4) "I'll go home and get my money," said Pedro.

(5) While Pedro was getting his money, Simon looked at his newly finished plane. He and Pedro had spent about four hours building it. Around an hour ago, Simon's father came upstairs with sandwiches and glasses of milk.

(6) "Thought you two would like something to eat," said Simon's father, placing the tray on Simon's bed. "I'd eat this away from the work area, though. You do not want to get modeling glue on your lunch."

(7) Simon and Pedro laughed while rushing to the bathroom to wash the glue from their hands. It was the first time Simon had ever built a model airplane without his father's help. His father had offered, but this time Simon said he wanted to try it on his own. Then, when Pedro asked to stay and work with him, Simon decided that he could use Pedro's help. Pedro read the directions and handed Simon parts while Simon looked over Pedro's shoulder at the plans and carefully glued the pieces in place. It was the hardest model Simon had ever built. Just then there was a knock on the door.

(8) "Can I come in?" asked Simon's father.

(9) "Sure," said Simon. "Check out the plane!"

(10) "Wow," said Simon's father quietly, looking closely at the finished model. "You and Pedro did a great job. It looks just like the real thing."

(11) At that moment it occurred to Simon that his father, behind the proud smile, might feel hurt because Simon let Pedro help him after telling his father he wanted to build it alone.

(12) "You're not mad?" Simon asked.

(13) "Mad?" asked Simon's father. "Mad? About what?"

(14) "That I asked Pedro to help me after you offered," said Simon, taking his eyes from his father's face and looking at the model.

(15) "Simon," said his father, "of course I'm not mad. I'm proud. You and Pedro did a great job! I think I can take some credit for teaching you, but this shows that you are ready to start tackling these kinds of projects on your own. Or, of course, with a friend."

(16) "Thanks, Dad," said Simon, giving his father a hug. "You did teach me a lot of things. I remembered a few of them when we were building the plane. Pedro knows a lot too. I'll probably get him to help me with the next model I build. Pedro's dad likes building models too."

(17) "Speaking of Pedro, there's the doorbell," said Simon's father, giving Simon a quick last squeeze. "Would you two like a ride to the store this time? Traffic is pretty heavy this time of day."

(18) "Yes, the traffic probably would be a lot worse now, so we could use a ride" said Simon. "Thanks, Dad."

(19) "No problem," said Simon's father. "I'll get the keys."

35. Why did Simon think his father would be angry?

a. Because Simon didn't buy the 1969 Mustang
b. Because Simon's father didn't want to help build the model
c. Because Simon and Pedro made a big mess
d. Because Simon asked Pedro instead of his father to help

36. Part A: What will Simon likely do the next time he builds a model?

a. Ask his father for help
b. Invite Pedro over to help
c. Read the directions more carefully
d. Build it alone

Part B: What sentence supports your answer in Part A?

a. I'll probably get him to help me with the next model I build.
b. I think I can take some credit for teaching you, but this shows that you are ready to start tackling these kinds of projects on your own.
c. I remembered a few of them when we were building the plane.
d. "Would you two like a ride to the store this time?

Questions 37–40 pertain to both passages: "Simon and Pedro's Shopping Trip" and "Simon and His Father":

37. From these two reading passages, it appears that Simon and Pedro are ____________.

a. Classmates
b. Enemies
c. Acquaintances
d. Friends

38. What kind of help does Simon accept from his father in "Simon and His Father"?

a. Simon lets his father drive him and Pedro to the store
b. Simon lets his father make dinner for him and Pedro
c. Simon lets his father help with Pedro's 1969 Mustang
d. Simon lets his father drive Pedro back to his house

39. What did Simon learn about his father in "Simon and His Father"? Select all the apply.

a. His father is a good cook.
b. His father is a good teacher.
c. His father understands that Simon and Pedro are friends.
d. His father understands that Simon is growing up.
e. His father values Simon gaining independence and skills.

40. Why does Simon accept his father's offer of help?

a. Because he was tired from the trip that morning
b. Because Pedro was taking a long time to get back
c. Because traffic in the afternoon is heavier than in the morning
d. Because it was getting late and the store was going to close soon

Answers and Explanations for Reading Test #2

1. B: The expression "rain came down in sheets" means it was raining so hard that the rain looked like it was coming down in one solid sheet rather than separate drops.

2. D: Mona and Yuri's mother was asleep after having worked overnight as a nurse.

3. C: Mona and Yuri's mother goes to bed around 7 a.m. after working all night. She usually gets up after eight hours of sleep, which would be around 3 p.m.

4. A: War is a card game. It can be played with an ordinary deck of playing cards.

5. A: When a regular deck of playing cards is used, an ace has the highest value in War and beats all other cards.

6. B: To have a "war" in the card game War, both players have to have the same card.

7. C: Mona won the first game that she and Yuri played. That is why Yuri said, "Beginner's luck."

8. A: When she said, "Actually, this game is all luck," Mona meant that the game did not require any skill to win. It just depended on the cards the players had.

9. A: Mona wins the round. A king is the second highest card in the deck. A jack is the fourth highest.

10. C: Gov. Richards taught social studies and history before getting into politics.

11. Part A: D: Paragraph 3 is mostly about Gov. Richards's achievements as governor of Texas.

Part B: A: This is the only answer choice that states one of her achievements from paragraph 3.

12. B: The word "styled" refers to how her hair was fixed.

13. A: Gov. Richards was joking about how stiff her hair was because of all the hairspray in it.

14. Part A: C: Sen. Hutchinson earned a law degree from the University of Texas in 1967.

Part B: D: The second sentence in paragraph 1 reads, "She went to the University of Texas and graduated with a law degree in 1967."

15. B: Sen. Hutchinson worked as a TV news reporter before going into politics.

16. Part A: D: Paragraph 3 is mostly about Sen. Hutchinson's accomplishments while serving as a senator.

Part B: A: Both of these examples from the passage best support that paragraph 3 is mainly about Senator Hutchinson's accomplishments.

17. A: The abbreviation Sen. means Senator.

18. B: Gov. Richards and Sen. Hutchinson were the first women to be governor and a US senator in Texas.

19. C: Both women served as the Texas State Treasurer before getting more important positions in government.

20. B: Sen. Hutchinson is still working as a US Senator. Gov. Richards died in 2006, and the passage states that she left politics.

21. A: The author wrote these articles to show that women can have the same opportunities as men in Texas.

22. B: Sam called Pavarti to get directions to Pavarti's house. Sam will give the directions to her mother when they drive over the next day.

23. A: Pavarti asked Sam where she lived so that she could give Sam directions from her own house.

24. D: Sam's mother will need to turn onto Elm Street after Townline Road.

25. A: Pavarti told Sam the color of her house and the houses around it because her address is hard to see from the road.

26. A: Sam's mother should go straight on Rio Turnpike before taking a right on Main Street.

27. C: Pavarti said to, "Look for either a red truck or a small black car."

28. B: Sam is hoping that her and her mother don't get lost and have to drive up and down Main Street, especially since it runs only one way.

29. D: Sam's notes written out would look like the following: *At the third traffic light you will turn left onto Rio Turnpike. Go about half a mile until you see a 7-Eleven on the right. The next street after the 7-Eleven is Main Street.*

30. D: After buying the pumpkins, Pavarti's family is planning to have lunch before starting to carve them.

31. Part A: C: Pedro noticed the model of the 1969 Mustang because his father had talked about that type of car.

Part B: B: In the story Pedro says that his grandfather had owned a real 1969 Mustang.

32. A: Simon wanted to buy a model of a C17 fighter plane, but he didn't have enough money.

33. B: Altogether, with tax, Simon had to pay $27.

34. C: After buying Simon's model, the B17G Flying Fortress, they planned to build it and then go buy the 1969 Mustang that Pedro wanted and build that one as well.

35. D: Simon turned down his father's offer of help, but accepted Pedro's.

36. Part A: B: It is likely that Simon will invite Pedro over to help the next time he builds a model airplane.

Part B: A: This is the sentence where he says that he will probably invite Pedro over to help.

37. D: The passage gives a strong indication that Simon and Pedro are friends.

38. A: Simon lets his father drive him and Pedro to the store to buy Pedro's model of a 1969 Mustang.

39. D, E: Simon learned from his father that he understands that Simon is growing up and relying less on his parents and more on his friends for help. He also learned that his father values Simon gaining independence and skills on his own.

40. C: Simon accepts a drive from his father because traffic is heavier in the afternoon than it is in the morning.

Language Practice Test #2

Questions 1-4 pertain to the following passage:

The Woman Who Made a Wizard

(1) In 1997, a new writer named J. K. Rowling amazed parents and teachers alike by inspiring young people to read. (2) She did this with the help of a young wizard named Harry Potter. (3) Rowling's book, *Harry Potter and the Philosopher's Stone*, was just the first in a series that would capture the world's imagination.

(4) Joanne Rowling was born near Gloucestershire, England, in 1965. (5) Originally, she was not able to get any of her stories published. (6) Then one day while riding a train, she got an idea. (7) She imagined a boy who seemed ordinary in every way. (8) But, little did he know, he had powers that were anything but ordinary. (9) In fact, little Harry Potter had such amazing powers that he was already famous in the world of his fellow wizards. (10) Suddenly, through her writing, Rowling threw this "normal" boy into a series of incredible adventures. (11) He faced all kinds of creatures, villains, and dangerous situations while making some loyal new friends along the way.

(12) This new idea and story became Rowling's first novel. (13) Although it was long, *Harry Potter and the Philosopher's Stone* became a major hit with young readers. (14) Harry did things next and they could not wait to find out what. (15) J. K. Rowling did not make them wait long. (16) She published *Harry Potter and the Chamber of Secrets* just a year after her first book. (17) Once again, the book was a success! (18) Later, Rowling followed the sequel with five more books in the series.

(19) The books became so popular that they were made into movies. (20) The first movie came out before the fifth book had even been published! (21) The film series ended with two movies based on the last one, *Harry Potter and the Deathly Hallows*. (22) While the movies were not perfect adaptations of the books, they introduced new fans to the story of Harry Potter. (23) The movies, like the books, won many awards and earned a large profit.

(24) In 2007, J. K. Rowling published her final Harry Potter book, *Harry Potter and the Deathly Hallows*. (25) By this point, both Harry and the readers who loved him had grown up. (26) Rowling was ready to move on too, announcing plans to not only write more children's books, but ones for adults, as well. (27) No matter what J.K. Rowling does next, she will always have many, many fans grateful that she created the most famous little wizard in modern literature.

1. Which of the following sentences would be an appropriate supporting detail to add after sentence 4?

a. Gloucestershire is located in the southern portion of England.
b. Her first child was born before the first *Harry Potter* book came out.
c. In the 1990s, she was a mother dreaming of a career as a writer.
d. She did not write Harry Potter until she was in her 30s.

2. Which of the following is the best way to revise sentence 14 to have a clear meaning?

a. Harry did things next, and they could not wait to find out what.
b. They could not wait to find out, and Harry did things next.
c. Harry did things next, yet they could not wait to find out what.
d. They could not wait to find out what Harry did next.

3. The transition at the beginning of sentence 18 is not very clear. Which of the following transitions should be used to make the sentence clearer?

a. After that
b. A while later
c. Over the next decade
d. In the future

4. Sentence 21 uses unclear wording. Choose the word that should be used instead of *one*.

a. book
b. movie
c. award
d. author

Questions 5-8 pertain to the following passage:

Walruses

(1) What is the funniest-looking animal on earth? (2) Well, there are a lot of funny-looking animals in the world, but without a doubt, one of the funniest-looking ones is the walrus. (3) They look funny when they're sitting around, they look funny when they're lying down, and they really look funny when they pull themselves out of the water or across the ice, using their long tusks to help them move. (4) In fact, walruses are so funny-looking that they're cute! (5) The walrus's scientific name is *Odobenus*, which is Latin for "tooth walker."

(6) Walruses are between 8 and 12 feet long and can weigh nearly 4,000 pounds. (7) They look like gargantuan balls of blubber with two gigantic teeth! (8) In fact, they really are gargantuan balls of blubber—under their skin is a layer of fat that is almost six inches thick. (9) This fat layer is like having a very thick swimsuit on. (10) It keeps them warm in the extremely frigid water where they obtain their food. (11) Their whiskers also contribute to their funny appearance, but they serve an important purpose: they help the walrus find its food. (12) Their tusks are around three feet long and are used for breaking ice, climbing out of the water, and fighting.

(13) Before, walruses have brown skin. (14) It turns lighter and lighter as they age, and the older ones look almost pink. (15) They usually live to be around 25 years old, but some can reach as old as 30. (16) Their main foods are small sea creatures such as shrimp, crabs, and clams, which they find on the bottom of the sea. (17) They use their whiskers to feel around for food on the seafloor, and they will force creatures out of hiding by spraying a mouthful of water in their direction. (18) They can stay underwater for long periods before coming up for air. (19) They can also float for hours at the surface because they have airbags under their throats.

(20) There aren't many animals that eat walruses, which is a good thing because they are so big that they can't move fast enough to get away from a predator. (21)

Polar bears and killer whales will attack walruses, but usually they eat young or injured ones. (22) An adult walrus can fight back hard. (23) Killer whales and polar bears prefer to avoid adult walruses if they can. (24) All in all, walruses have a pretty nice life. (25) They get to spend their days swimming in the ocean or lying in the sun, and they have all the food they want for free. (26) The only things they really have to worry about are killer whales and polar bears. (27) Most animals would love to have such an easy life. (28) So, walruses might be funny-looking, but they're the ones who have the last laugh!

5. One of the sentences in the first paragraph contains unnecessary information and should be removed. Which sentence should be removed?

a. Sentence 1
b. Sentence 2
c. Sentence 3
d. Sentence 5

6. Which sentence should be added before sentence 6 to improve the transition into the second paragraph?

a. Many animals have tusks, but they do not look very funny.
b. Besides being funny-looking, walruses are also huge.
c. While walruses can be cute, they can also be dangerous
d. Some adult walruses look pink instead of brown.

7. A clearer transition is needed at the beginning of sentence 13. Which phrase should be used to replace before?

a. When they are young
b. A little earlier
c. For a while
d. Until it is time

8. Which of the following is the best way to combine sentences 22 and 23?

a. An adult walrus can fight back hard, killer whales and polar bears prefer to avoid them if they can.
b. An adult walrus can fight back hard, so killer whales and polar bears prefer to avoid them if they can.
c. An adult walrus can fight back hard and killer whales and polar bears prefer to avoid adult walruses if they can.
d. An adult walrus can fight back hard; preferring to avoid adult walruses if they can, killer whales and polar bears.

Questions 9-11 pertain to the following passage:

Finding Maize

(1) My name is Tanya, and I have a dog whose name is Maize. (2) I found her one summer outside of the supermarket. (3) She were a puppy at the time. (4) I was taking our cart back to the store when I saw a small, black and white animal dart under a row of shopping carts next to the main door. (5) It moved so fast! (6) All I saw was a blur. (7) I did not know if the animal was a cat, a dog, or a skunk until it started barkeeng.

(8) My mom always told me not to play with strange animals, but something about Maize seemed safe. (9) I bent down to look for her under the carts and called to her. (10) She came creepping out, slowly at first. (11) Then she ran straight to me, wagging her tail. (12) I picked her up and brought her back to my mom.

9. Which change would correct the mistake in sentence 3?

a. Change *She* to *Her*.
b. Change *were* to *was*.
c. Add a comma after *puppy*.
d. Change *time* to *tym*.

10. Which change would correct the mistake in sentence 7?

a. Change *did not know* to *did not knew*.
b. Remove the comma after *dog*.
c. Change *barkeeng* to *barking*.
d. No change is needed in sentence 7.

11. Which change would correct the mistake in sentence 10?

a. Change *came* to *come*.
b. Change *creepping* to *creeping*.
c. Change *slowly* to *quickly*.
d. Change *at* to *from*.

Questions 12-15 pertain to the following passage:

Roger Staubach

(1) There are many figures in sports histery that stand out as remarkable, but few can compare to former Dallas Cowboys quarterback Roger Staubach. (2) He was born on February 5, 1942 in Cincinnati, Ohio. (3) Once he attended high school, Staubach enrolled in the United States Naval Academy. (4) As a sophomore in the Naval Academy, Staubach became the Navy's starting quarterback. (5) In his junior year at the Naval Academy, he led the teams to a number-two ranking, losing the Cotton Bowl to number-two-ranked Texas. (6) The Navy's team also defeated Notre Dame, one of their fiercest rivals. (7) That year, Staubach won the Heisman Trophy, which is awarded to the best college football player in America.

(8) Staubach was a 10th-round draft pick of the Dallas Cowboys in the 1964 National Football League (NFL) draft. (9) However, he couldn't start playing professionally right away. (10) As a graduate of the US Naval Academy, he was obligated to serve in the Navy for several years after graduation. (11) Finally, in 1969, he arrived at the Dallas Cowboys training camp just in time to be able to play as a 27-year-old rookie.

12. Which change would correct the mistake in sentence 1?

a. Add a comma after *figures.*
b. Change *histery* to *history*.
c. Change *but* to *and.*
d. Change *Dallas Cowboys* to *Dallas cowboys.*

13. Which word should be used in place of Once in sentence 3?

_______ he attended high school, Staubach enrolled in the United States Naval Academy.
When
As
After
Until

14. Which change would correct the mistake in sentence 5?

a. Change *In* to *Through.*
b. Remove the comma after *Academy.*
c. Change *led* to *leads.*
d. Change *teams* to *team.*

15. Which change would correct the mistake in sentence 9?

a. Change *he* to *him.*
b. Change *couldn't* to *can't.*
c. Change *professionally* to *profeshionally*.
d. No change is needed in sentence 9.

Questions 16-19 pertain to the following passage:

The Beginnings of Basketball

(1) One of the most popular and exciting sports of our time is basketball. (2) Behind this fast-paced sport is a rich history. (3) The game has changed many times over the years, but the basics remain the same. (4) From its humble beginnings in 1891, basketball has grown to have worldwide appeal.

(5) In 1891, Dr. James Naismith, a teacher and minister, was responsible for a group of college students at the Springfield YMCA Training School in Springfield, Massachusetts. (6) He needed an indoor game to keep them busy during the long winter days. (7) This need prompted the creation of basketball. (8) The game was originally played by tossing a soccer ball into an empty peach basket nailed to the gym wall. (9) It is not known where the peach basket came from. (10) Additionally, the original game involved two teams and only one basket.

(11) Because basketball was so simple, the game spread across the nation within 30 years of its invention. (12) As more basketball teams formed, it became clear that a league was needed. (13) On June 6, 1946, the Basketball Association of America (BAA) was formed. (14) The smaller National Basketball League (NBL) formed soon after. (15) In 1948, the BAA merged with the NBL, and the National Basketball Association (NBA) was born. (16) The NBA played its first full season in 1948–49.

(17) The National Basketball Association is the only major basketball league in America. (18) There are 30 NBA teams across the country. (19) The teams in the league compete in an annual tournament. (20) Millions of Americans watch the tournament on television and in person. (21) The NBA makes billions of dollars annually.

(22) Though much has changed in our world since 1891, the popularity of basketball has remained strong. (23) From its humble start in a YMCA gym to the multi-million-dollar empire it is today, the simple fun of the sport has endured. (24) Although many changes have been made over the years, the essence of basketball has remained constant. (25) Its rich history and simplicity ensure that basketball will always be a popular sport around the world.

16. There is an unnecessary sentence in paragraph 2. Which sentence from paragraph 2 should be removed?

a. Sentence 6
b. Sentence 7
c. Sentence 9
d. Sentence 10

17. Which of the following transition words would be best to add at the beginning of sentence 17?

a. Today
b. Eventually
c. Shortly
d. Meanwhile

18. Which of the following correctly combines sentences 19 and 20?

a. The teams in the league compete in an annual tournament, millions of Americans watch it on television and in person.
b. Teams in the league compete in an annual tournament and millions of Americans watch it on television and in person.
c. The teams in the league compete in an annual tournament, and millions of Americans watch it on television and in person.
d. The teams in the league compete in an annual tournament when millions of Americans watch on television and in person.

19. Which of the following sentences should be added after sentence 21 to conclude the fourth paragraph?

a. Tickets to the tournament can be expensive, but many fans are willing to pay to go watch the games.
b. The NBA has grown into a billion-dollar organization since it was created in the mid-twentieth century.
c. Basketball is also played in local leagues and minor leagues, and it has even become an Olympic sport.
d. All of these impressive statistics were made possible because of Dr. Naismith's creative thinking.

Questions 20-22 pertain to the following passage:

The Treasure that is Tennis

(1) Though tennis has been around for centuries, it is still a popular sport today. (2) Professionals and casual players alike can be found serving and volleying on tennis courts around the world. (3) In fact, Wimbledon, one of the most famous tennis tournaments, includes participants from over 50 different countries. (4) It has also been won by players from several different countries. (5) The tournament is attended by thousands of tennis fans each year and is organized by the All England Lawn Tennis and Croquet Club, or the AEltC.

(6) Tennis can be played one-on-one or in teams of two. (7) Tennis is played on a court that is painted with lines and includes a net. (8) Players take turns hitting the ball. (9) While a player hits the ball, the ball has to go over the net and land within the lines. (10) If it does not go over the net or lands outside of the lines, the other player or team wins the point. (11) The player must promptly return the ball, or hit it, after their opponent has hit it over the net. (12) If the player fails to return the ball before it bounces twice, then the player's opponent wins that point. (13) The second bounce may occur everywhere, including outside of the lines, so players must be prepared to move quickly.

20. Which change would correct the mistake in sentence 5?

a. Change *is* to *was.*
b. Change *attended by* to *attended for.*
c. Change *organized* to *orgenized.*
d. Change *AEltC* to *AELTC.*

21. Which change would correct the mistake in sentence 9?

a. Change *While* to *After*.
b. Change *has* to *have*.
c. Change *land* to *will land*.
d. Add a comma after *land*.

22. Select the correct pronoun to use in sentence 13.

The second bounce may occur ____________, including outside of the lines, so players must be prepared to move quickly.

everywhere
nowhere
anywhere
somewhere

Questions 23-28 pertain to the following passage:

A Dreamer Named George Lucas

(1) You may not know the name George Lucas, but you probably know the incredible world he created. He is the mastermind behind such beloved heroes as Luke Skywalker, R2-D2, Chewbacca, and Queen Amidala. He also created such dreaded villains as Darth Vader, Boba Fett, and Emperor Palpatine. These are some of the main characters in the wildly popular series of movies called *Star Wars*. And none of these films would exist if not for a young dreamer from Modesto, California.

(2) George Lucas was born on May 14, 1944. As a young man, George loved driving his car around Modesto and dreamed of becoming a racecar driver. However, he became interested in film while studying at junior college. He focused on film while at the University of Southern California School of Cinematic Arts, where he learned the skills that would make him famous.

(3) At the university, George made his first film. It was a science-fiction story called *THX 1138*. A friend of his thought the film was too serious. He challenged George to make a lighthearted comedy. George rose to the challenge by making a movie called *American Graffiti*. The movie was about a group of teenagers who liked nothing better than driving around town in their cars. The story was not very dramatic. The movie studio was concerned that people would not be interested in his film. But audiences related to the funny, likable characters, and the film became a big hit. George's success with *American Graffiti* meant he would be able to make more films.

(4) For his next project, he returned to science fiction. But instead of making another serious, adult film like *THX 1138*, he decided to make one with the lighthearted, fast-paced feel of *American Graffiti*. Once again, the studio executives were worried that audiences would not like George's space adventure. They thought his world of creatures and robots was too strange. Once again, the studio was wrong. Released in 1977, *Star Wars* made more money than any movie before it. George was right again.

(5) George Lucas spent the next few years working on sequels to his big hit. *The Empire Strikes Back* was released in 1980. *Return of the Jedi* followed in 1983. In the meantime, he created a new character, an adventurer named Indiana Jones. Indiana

would go on to star in five popular movies of his own. It seemed that George could only have success, but making these films was a lot of hard work. He decided to take some time off from making movies, although he promised fans that there were more stories to tell in the *Star Wars* universe.

(6) Sixteen years later, George Lucas finally returned to the most successful series in movie history. But instead of picking up where *Return of the Jedi* ended, he decided to tell the story of what happened before the first *Star Wars* movie he made. *The Phantom Menace* was released in 1999. Then came *Attack of the Clones* in 2002 and *Revenge of the Sith* in 2005.

(7) When he isn't making blockbusters, George Lucas likes to spend time with his family. He even allowed his three children to appear in his most recent *Star Wars* movies. Who knows what he will dream up next?

23. Which of the following sentences from the passage is a compound sentence? Select all that apply.

a. You may not know the name George Lucas, but you probably know the incredible world he created.
b. As a young man, George loved driving his car around Modesto and dreamed of becoming a racecar driver.
c. Sixteen years later, George Lucas finally returned to the most successful series in movie history.
d. It seemed that George could only have success, but making these films was a lot of hard work.
e. For his next project, he returned to science fiction.

24. Which revision best improves the clarity of the following sentence?

"He even allowed his three children to appear in his most recent *Star Wars* movies."

a. "He allowed, even his three children, to appear in his most recent *Star Wars* movies."
b. "Even his three children appeared in the most recent *Star Wars* movies, allowed by him."
c. "His three children even got to appear in his most recent *Star Wars* movies."
d. "His three children were allowed to appear in the *Star Wars* movies that were most recent."

25. What is the best way to revise the following sentences?

"*The Phantom Menace* was released in 1999. Then came *Attack of the Clones* in 2002 and *Revenge of the Sith* in 2005."

a. *The Phantom Menace* was released in 1999, followed by *Attack of the Clones* in 2002 and *Revenge of the Sith* in 2005.
b. The *Phantom Menace* was released in 1999, *Attack of the Clones* in 2002 and *Revenge of the Sith* in 2005.
c. *The Phantom Menace* was released in 1999, followed by *Attack of the Clones* was released in 2002 and *Revenge of the Sith* was released in 2005.
d. In 1999, *The Phantom Menace* was released, in 2002 *Attack of the Clones*, and in 2005 *Revenge of the Sith*.

26. Which of the following ways correctly revises the error in the following sentence?

"But instead of picking up where *Return of the Jedi* ended, he decided to tell the story of what happened before the first *Star Wars* movie he made."

a. But, instead of picking up where *Return of the Jedi* ended, he decided to tell the story of what happened before the first *Star Wars* movie he made.
b. But instead of picking up where *Return of the Jedi* ended he decided to tell the story of what happened before the first *Star Wars* movie he made.
c. Instead of picking up where *Return of the Jedi* ended, he decided to tell the story of what happened before the first *Star Wars* movie he made.
d. No change needed.

27. The passage "A Dreamer Named George Lucas" is best described as what type of text?

a. Narrative
b. Expository
c. Persuasive
d. Instructional

28. What is the best way to combine the following two sentences?

"These are some of the main characters in the wildly popular series of movies called *Star Wars*. And none of these films would exist if not for a young dreamer from Modesto, California.

a. None of these characters from the wildly popular series of movies called *Star Wars* would exist if not for young dreamer from Modesto, California.
b. These are some of the main characters in the wildly popular series of movies called *Star Wars*, and none of these films would exist if not for a young dreamer from Modesto, California.
c. These are some of the main characters that would not exist if not for a young dreamer from Modesto, California.
d. These popular characters from *Star Wars* would not exist if not for a young dreamer.

Answers and Explanations for Language Test #2

1. C: Sentence 4 explains when and where J.K. Rowling was born. Sentence 5 states that she was not able to get her stories published. A sentence added after sentence 4 should connect these ideas. Since sentence 5 is about Rowling trying to get her stories published, the new sentence should mention her writing. Choice C is the best choice because it shows that Rowling was dreaming of becoming a writer. This connects sentences 4 and 5 by showing what happened after she grew up and why she wanted to get her stories published. Choice A is incorrect because it gives unnecessary information. Choice B is incorrect because it does not connect the ideas in sentences 4 and 5. Choice D is incorrect because it gives information in the incorrect order. Rowling wrote *Harry Potter* after the event in sentence 6, so the sentence in choice D would come after sentence 6.

2. D: Sentence 14 is not clear because it gives information in an order that is hard to understand. It states that Harry continued to do things, and it states that readers wanted to know something. Readers wanted to find out what Harry did next. The sentence should be complete, clear, and grammatically correct. The other sentences do not provide any clarity, or they do not make sense.

3. C: The transition at the beginning of sentence 18 is vague, or unclear. A more specific transition would help the reader understand how much time it took for Rowling to complete the *Harry Potter* series. Choice C is correct because it gives a specific amount of time. Choices A and D are incorrect because they are also unclear. They have the same meaning as *later*, which means that they do not give the reader any more information. While choice B is more specific than *later* and shows that a long amount of time passed, it is not as specific as choice C.

4. A: Sentence 21 says that two movies were made based on *Harry Potter and the Deathly Hallows*. This is the name of the last book in the *Harry Potter* series. Sentences 19 and 22 show that the movies were based on the books in the *Harry Potter* series. This shows that choice A is correct, since the last two movies in the film series were based on the last book. Choice B is incorrect because the movies were not based on the others in the film series. Choice C is incorrect because, while the passage says that the movies won awards, it does not support the idea that they were based on awards. Choice D is incorrect because there is only one author mentioned in this passage. The word *one* in sentence 21 cannot be replaced with *author* because there would need to be more than one author in order for there to be a last author.

5. D: Sentence 5 should be removed because it gives distracting and unnecessary information. Paragraph 1 introduces the topic and describes the appearance of walruses. Each sentence in the paragraph should support this topic and help create a transition into the next paragraph. Choice D is correct because the information in sentence 5 is unnecessary. The information in sentence 5 repeats information from sentence 3 and does not support sentence 4. It also does not create an effective transition to the next paragraph. Choice A is incorrect because sentence 1 prepares the reader for the rest of the information in the paragraph. Choice B is incorrect because sentence 2 introduces the topic of the passage and supports sentence 1. Choice C is incorrect because sentence 3 gives the reader the needed information and supports sentence 2.

6. B: Choice B is correct because it creates a clear transition from paragraph 1 to paragraph 2. It mentions that walruses look funny and adds that they are also very big. This helps the reader see the connection between the two paragraphs and shows what paragraph 2 is about. Choices A and B are incorrect because they are not related to the topic of the second paragraph. Choice D is incorrect because it is related to paragraph 3, not paragraph 2.

7. A: The transition word *before* is not clear and does not help the reader understand when walruses have brown skin. Choice A is correct because it is specific and helps the reader understand when walruses begin to change color. Choices B and C are incorrect because they are unclear. They do not provide enough information to help the reader understand the meaning of sentence 13. Choice D is more specific than choices B and C, but it still does not help the reader understand when in a walrus's life its coloring will change.

8. B: The new sentence should include the information given in both sentence 22 and sentence 23. Sentence 22 says that an adult walrus is able to fight back if it is attacked. Sentence 23 says that killer whales and polar bears try to stay away from walruses. This suggests that these predators avoid walruses because walruses can fight back. The sentence should be complete, clear, and free of any grammatical errors. Answer choice A uses a comma splice. Answer choice C is a run-on sentence. Answer choice D has a misplaced modifier and sounds very awkward in phrasing.

9. B: *Were* is a plural verb that is used to describe the action done by a plural noun or pronoun. Since *She* is a singular pronoun, a singular verb should be used. *Were* should be changed to *was*, which is a singular noun. Choice B is correct. *She* is a subjective pronoun, and *her* is an objective pronoun. The word *she* is currently the subject of sentence 3. Since the subject should be a noun or subjective pronoun, *she* is used correctly, and choice B is incorrect. There is no need to add a comma after *puppy*, since commas are not always added before prepositional phrases, so choice C is incorrect. The word *time* is spelled using a silent *-e*. The word is spelled correctly in sentence 3, so choice D is incorrect.

10. C: The word *barking* is spelled incorrectly in sentence 7. *Barking* is spelled using the verb *bark* and the suffix *-ing*. Since this word uses the suffix *-ing*, it is not spelled *barkeeng*, so choice C is correct. *Know* is a present tense verb, and *knew* is a past tense verb. However, the words *did not* are used before *know* in sentence 7. Since the word *did* is a past tense verb, it makes the phrase *did not know* function as a past tense verb. *Know* does not need to be changed to *knew*, so choice A is incorrect. The word *dog* is the second item in a list of three items. It comes before *and*, so it should be followed by a comma. Choice B is incorrect. Choice D is incorrect because *barkeeng* should be changed to *barking.*

11. B: The word *creeping* is spelled using the verb *creep* and the suffix *-ing*. Sometimes, when adding a suffix to a word that ends in a consonant, the consonant must be doubled. Usually, the consonant is doubled when the suffix begins with a vowel and the root word ends with a single vowel followed by a single consonant. In this case, *creep* is spelled using two vowels before the last consonant. This means that the consonant *p* does not need to be doubled when the suffix *-ing* is added to *creep*. Choice B is correct, since *creepping* is misspelled. *Came* is a is a past tense verb, and *come* is a present tense verb. Sentence 10 is in the past tense, so it should be written using past tense verbs. *Came* is used correctly in sentence 10, so choice A is incorrect. Choices C and D suggest changing words in ways that would change the meaning of the sentence. The sentence makes sense, and the words *slowly* and *at* are used correctly, so choices C and D are incorrect.

12. B: *Histery* is a misspelling for the word *history*, so choice B is correct. The word *figures* is used before a prepositional phrase. While commas are often used after prepositional phrases, they are not needed before them, so choice A is incorrect. The first independent clause says there are many remarkable athletes in history. The second independent clause says that Roger Staubach is better than they are. The best coordinating conjunction to use between these sentences is one that shows contrast. *But* is the correct conjunction to use in sentence 1, so choice C is incorrect. The Dallas Cowboys are a football team, and their team's name is a proper noun. All the nouns in a proper noun should be capitalized, so choice D is incorrect.

13. After: This sentence describes what Roger Staubach did following his time in high school, so *after* is the best word to use at the beginning of this sentence. Using *when* or *as* would suggest that he went to high school and was in the Navy at the same time. This is not what the sentence should say, so those choices are incorrect. *Until* suggests that he joined the Navy before he was in high school. This is also not what the sentence should say, so it is an incorrect choice.

14. D: The word *team* is a collective noun. This means that it is a singular noun that represents multiple members. So, even though there are multiple players on a team, the word *team* is singular, so it does not need to include an *s* at the end. Choice D is correct. *Through* would not make sense as the first word in sentence 5, so choice A is incorrect. The word *Academy* is the last word in a prepositional phrase. When a long prepositional phrase starts a sentence, it should be followed by a comma, so choice B is incorrect. *Led* is a past tense verb, and *leads* is a present tense verb. Sentence 5 is in the past tense, so *led* is used correctly, and choice C is incorrect.

15. D: This sentence does not contain any spelling or grammar errors, so choice D is correct. *He* is a subjective pronoun, and *him* is an objective pronoun. The word *he* is used as the subject of sentence 9, so it is used correctly, and choice A is incorrect. When used in a statement, *couldn't* is a contraction for the past tense verb phrase *could not. Can't* is a contraction for *cannot*, which is used in present tense sentences. Sentence 9 is in the past tense, so *couldn't* is used correctly, and choice B is incorrect. In the word *professionally*, the *ss* is pronounced like *sh*, though it is spelled *ss*. *Professionally* is spelled correctly, so choice C is incorrect.

16. C: Sentence 9 contains information that is unnecessary, so it should be removed. Therefore, choice C is correct. The fact that no one knows where the peach basket came from does not help the reader understand the other information in the paragraph. Choice A is incorrect because sentence 6 tells why Dr. Naismith invented the new game. This information is important to the passage and supports the information in sentence 5. Choice B is incorrect because sentence 7 explains how the information in sentence 6 is connected to the creation of basketball. Choice D is incorrect because sentence 10 gives information that helps the reader understand how the early version of basketball was played.

17. A: The third paragraph explains how the NBA, the biggest national basketball league, was created. Sentence 17 states that the National Basketball Association (NBA) is a major sports league. However, in sentence 16, the NBA had just been established. At the time, it was not a major sports league. A transition at the beginning of sentence 17 should show that time has passed, as sentence 17 is talking about the NBA today. Choice A is correct because adding *today* at the beginning of sentence 17 shows the reader that the NBA has changed between 1948 and today. Choice B is incorrect because it is not clear and would make the sentence grammatically incorrect. It shows that time passed before the NBA became a major league, but it does not show whether a small or large amount of time has passed. Choice C suggests that a short amount of time passed between the two events. This is not supported by the passage, so choice C is incorrect. Choice D is incorrect because it suggests that the NBA became the only major basketball league in America at the same time that it was established. This is not supported by the passage.

18. C: Choice C includes all of the information from sentences 19 and 20, is clear, and has no grammatical errors, so it is correct. Choice A is incorrect because it contains a comma splice. This means that it joins two independent clauses with a comma, but it does not contain a coordinating conjunction. Choice B is incorrect because it is a run-on sentence. Choice D is incorrect because it changes the meaning of sentences 19 and 20. Choice D says that the teams play in the tournament when millions of Americans watch. This suggests that the people watching are causing the teams to play in the tournament. This is not true since the teams playing in the tournament cause people to watch.

19. D: Choice D is correct because it shows the connection between the information in sentences 17 through 20 and the central idea of the passage. It also provides a transition from sentence 21 to sentence 22. Choice A is incorrect because it adds a new detail that does not support sentence 21 or create a transition. While it is related to money, it only explains part of the reason that the NBA makes so much money. Choice B is incorrect because it simply restates information given in sentences 15 and 21. Choice C is incorrect because it does not support the information in sentence 21 or create a transition to sentence 22.

20. D: In initialisms, the capitalization of each letter should match the way the words are capitalized in the full title or name. The initialism for the All England Lawn Tennis and Croquet Club should be AELTC, not AEltC, so choice D is correct. *Is* is a present tense verb, and *was* is a past tense verb. Sentence 5 is in the present tense, so it is used correctly, and choice A is incorrect. The phrase "attended by" refers to the people that went to the tournament. "Attended for" would refer to the reason the people went to the tournament. The sentence says, "The tournament is attended by thousands of tennis fans." Since the fans are the people that went to the game, "attended by" is the best phrase to use in sentence 10. Choice B is incorrect. *Orgenized* is a misspelling of *organized*, so choice C is incorrect.

21. A: The word *while* shows that two events happen at the same time. Sentence 9 describes what has to happen once a player hits the ball. Since the player has to hit the ball for the ball to go over the net, the ball cannot go over the net at the same time that the player is hitting it. The ball goes over the net after the player hits it, so choice A is correct. *Has* is a singular verb, and *have* is a plural verb. Ball is a singular noun, so it should be used with a singular verb, such as *has*. Since *has* is used correctly in sentence 9, choice B is incorrect. The word *will* is used before a verb to show that the action is going to happen. It is not certain that the ball will land within the lines. The sentence simply says that the ball has to land inside the lines. Choice C is incorrect. Commas are not usually needed before prepositional phrases that are used at the end of a sentence. No comma is needed after land, so choice D is incorrect.

22. anywhere: Sentence 13 describes where the second bounce of a tennis ball can happen. *Everywhere* should not be used in this sentence because *everywhere* refers to all the areas of the tennis court. It is impossible for one bounce to occur everywhere at once. The second bounce can happen at any location on the tennis court or the areas surrounding it. This means that the bounce can occur anywhere, so *anywhere* should be used in the blank. The bounce cannot occur nowhere because that would mean that it did not happen at all. *Nowhere* is incorrect. While the bounce must occur somewhere, using the word *somewhere* in the blank does not help the reader understand the rule that the sentence is describing. *Somewhere* is not specific enough, so it is incorrect.

23. A, D: A compound sentence has at least two independent clauses joined by a comma and conjunction or a semicolon. Answer choices A and D are the only sentences where this occurs. Answer choice B uses a conjunction, but it does not have two independent clauses and a comma before the conjunction. Answer choices C and E both begin with a dependent clause to add more clarification to the independent clause.

24. C: The most concise version that improves clarify is answer choice C. The other three answer choices add clarification statements in weird locations of the sentence.

25. A: Combining the two sentences helps with redundancy and clarity. However, answer choice A is the only option that does this correctly.

26. C: Starting the sentence with a conjunction is not proper. Answer choice C is the only option that does not start the sentence with the word "but."

27. B: An expository text provides factual information in a clear, informative way. It does not tell a fictional narrative, and it does not argue a point. The structure is chronological, but it does not list a bunch of steps to be carried out.

28. A: The best way to combine these sentences is answer choice A. While answer choice B is also an acceptable way to combine the sentences, it is not as concise as answer choice A. The other two answer choices leave out important details from both sentences.

How to Overcome Test Anxiety

Just the thought of taking a test is enough to make most people a little nervous. A test is an important event that can have a long-term impact on your future, so it's important to take it seriously and it's natural to feel anxious about performing well. But just because anxiety is normal, that doesn't mean that it's helpful in test taking, or that you should simply accept it as part of your life. Anxiety can have a variety of effects. These effects can be mild, like making you feel slightly nervous, or severe, like blocking your ability to focus or remember even a simple detail.

If you experience test anxiety—whether severe or mild—it's important to know how to beat it. To discover this, first you need to understand what causes test anxiety.

Causes of Test Anxiety

While we often think of anxiety as an uncontrollable emotional state, it can actually be caused by simple, practical things. One of the most common causes of test anxiety is that a person does not feel adequately prepared for their test. This feeling can be the result of many different issues such as poor study habits or lack of organization, but the most common culprit is time management. Starting to study too late, failing to organize your study time to cover all of the material, or being distracted while you study will mean that you're not well prepared for the test. This may lead to cramming the night before, which will cause you to be physically and mentally exhausted for the test. Poor time management also contributes to feelings of stress, fear, and hopelessness as you realize you are not well prepared but don't know what to do about it.

Other times, test anxiety is not related to your preparation for the test but comes from unresolved fear. This may be a past failure on a test, or poor performance on tests in general. It may come from comparing yourself to others who seem to be performing better or from the stress of living up to expectations. Anxiety may be driven by fears of the future—how failure on this test would affect your educational and career goals. These fears are often completely irrational, but they can still negatively impact your test performance.

Elements of Test Anxiety

As mentioned earlier, test anxiety is considered to be an emotional state, but it has physical and mental components as well. Sometimes you may not even realize that you are suffering from test anxiety until you notice the physical symptoms. These can include trembling hands, rapid heartbeat, sweating, nausea, and tense muscles. Extreme anxiety may lead to fainting or vomiting. Obviously, any of these symptoms can have a negative impact on testing. It is important to recognize them as soon as they begin to occur so that you can address the problem before it damages your performance.

The mental components of test anxiety include trouble focusing and inability to remember learned information. During a test, your mind is on high alert, which can help you recall information and stay focused for an extended period of time. However, anxiety interferes with your mind's natural processes, causing you to blank out, even on the questions you know well. The strain of testing during anxiety makes it difficult to stay focused, especially on a test that may take several hours. Extreme anxiety can take a huge mental toll, making it difficult not only to recall test information but even to understand the test questions or pull your thoughts together.

Effects of Test Anxiety

Test anxiety is like a disease—if left untreated, it will get progressively worse. Anxiety leads to poor performance, and this reinforces the feelings of fear and failure, which in turn lead to poor performances on subsequent tests. It can grow from a mild nervousness to a crippling condition. If allowed to progress, test anxiety can have a big impact on your schooling, and consequently on your future.

Test anxiety can spread to other parts of your life. Anxiety on tests can become anxiety in any stressful situation, and blanking on a test can turn into panicking in a job situation. But fortunately, you don't have to let anxiety rule your testing and determine your grades. There are a number of relatively simple steps you can take to move past anxiety and function normally on a test and in the rest of life.

Physical Steps for Beating Test Anxiety

While test anxiety is a serious problem, the good news is that it can be overcome. It doesn't have to control your ability to think and remember information. While it may take time, you can begin taking steps today to beat anxiety.

Just as your first hint that you may be struggling with anxiety comes from the physical symptoms, the first step to treating it is also physical. Rest is crucial for having a clear, strong mind. If you are tired, it is much easier to give in to anxiety. But if you establish good sleep habits, your body and mind will be ready to perform optimally, without the strain of exhaustion. Additionally, sleeping well helps you to retain information better, so you're more likely to recall the answers when you see the test questions.

Getting good sleep means more than going to bed on time. It's important to allow your brain time to relax. Take study breaks from time to time so it doesn't get overworked, and don't study right before bed. Take time to rest your mind before trying to rest your body, or you may find it difficult to fall asleep.

Along with sleep, other aspects of physical health are important in preparing for a test. Good nutrition is vital for good brain function. Sugary foods and drinks may give a burst of energy but this burst is followed by a crash, both physically and emotionally. Instead, fuel your body with protein and vitamin-rich foods.

Also, drink plenty of water. Dehydration can lead to headaches and exhaustion, especially if your brain is already under stress from the rigors of the test. Particularly if your test is a long one, drink water during the breaks. And if possible, take an energy-boosting snack to eat between sections.

Along with sleep and diet, a third important part of physical health is exercise. Maintaining a steady workout schedule is helpful, but even taking 5-minute study breaks to walk can help get your blood pumping faster and clear your head. Exercise also releases endorphins, which contribute to a positive feeling and can help combat test anxiety.

When you nurture your physical health, you are also contributing to your mental health. If your body is healthy, your mind is much more likely to be healthy as well. So take time to rest, nourish your body with healthy food and water, and get moving as much as possible. Taking these physical steps will make you stronger and more able to take the mental steps necessary to overcome test anxiety.

Mental Steps for Beating Test Anxiety

Working on the mental side of test anxiety can be more challenging, but as with the physical side, there are clear steps you can take to overcome it. As mentioned earlier, test anxiety often stems from lack of preparation, so the obvious solution is to prepare for the test. Effective studying may be the most important weapon you have for beating test anxiety, but you can and should employ several other mental tools to combat fear.

First, boost your confidence by reminding yourself of past success—tests or projects that you aced. If you're putting as much effort into preparing for this test as you did for those, there's no reason you should expect to fail here. Work hard to prepare; then trust your preparation.

Second, surround yourself with encouraging people. It can be helpful to find a study group, but be sure that the people you're around will encourage a positive attitude. If you spend time with others who are anxious or cynical, this will only contribute to your own anxiety. Look for others who are motivated to study hard from a desire to succeed, not from a fear of failure.

Third, reward yourself. A test is physically and mentally tiring, even without anxiety, and it can be helpful to have something to look forward to. Plan an activity following the test, regardless of the outcome, such as going to a movie or getting ice cream.

When you are taking the test, if you find yourself beginning to feel anxious, remind yourself that you know the material. Visualize successfully completing the test. Then take a few deep, relaxing breaths and return to it. Work through the questions carefully but with confidence, knowing that you are capable of succeeding.

Developing a healthy mental approach to test taking will also aid in other areas of life. Test anxiety affects more than just the actual test—it can be damaging to your mental health and even contribute to depression. It's important to beat test anxiety before it becomes a problem for more than testing.

Study Strategy

Being prepared for the test is necessary to combat anxiety, but what does being prepared look like? You may study for hours on end and still not feel prepared. What you need is a strategy for test prep. The next few pages outline our recommended steps to help you plan out and conquer the challenge of preparation.

Step 1: Scope Out the Test

Learn everything you can about the format (multiple choice, essay, etc.) and what will be on the test. Gather any study materials, course outlines, or sample exams that may be available. Not only will this help you to prepare, but knowing what to expect can help to alleviate test anxiety.

Step 2: Map Out the Material

Look through the textbook or study guide and make note of how many chapters or sections it has. Then divide these over the time you have. For example, if a book has 15 chapters and you have five days to study, you need to cover three chapters each day. Even better, if you have the time, leave an extra day at the end for overall review after you have gone through the material in depth.

If time is limited, you may need to prioritize the material. Look through it and make note of which sections you think you already have a good grasp on, and which need review. While you are studying, skim quickly through the familiar sections and take more time on the challenging parts.

Write out your plan so you don't get lost as you go. Having a written plan also helps you feel more in control of the study, so anxiety is less likely to arise from feeling overwhelmed at the amount to cover.

Step 3: Gather Your Tools

Decide what study method works best for you. Do you prefer to highlight in the book as you study and then go back over the highlighted portions? Or do you type out notes of the important information? Or is it helpful to make flashcards that you can carry with you? Assemble the pens, index cards, highlighters, post-it notes, and any other materials you may need so you won't be distracted by getting up to find things while you study.

If you're having a hard time retaining the information or organizing your notes, experiment with different methods. For example, try color-coding by subject with colored pens, highlighters, or post-it notes. If you learn better by hearing, try recording yourself reading your notes so you can listen while in the car, working out, or simply sitting at your desk. Ask a friend to quiz you from your flashcards, or try teaching someone the material to solidify it in your mind.

Step 4: Create Your Environment

It's important to avoid distractions while you study. This includes both the obvious distractions like visitors and the subtle distractions like an uncomfortable chair (or a too-comfortable couch that makes you want to fall asleep). Set up the best study environment possible: good lighting and a comfortable work area. If background music helps you focus, you may want to turn it on, but otherwise keep the room quiet. If you are using a computer to take notes, be sure you don't have any other windows open, especially applications like social media, games, or anything else that could distract you. Silence your phone and turn off notifications. Be sure to keep water close by so you stay hydrated while you study (but avoid unhealthy drinks and snacks).

Also, take into account the best time of day to study. Are you freshest first thing in the morning? Try to set aside some time then to work through the material. Is your mind clearer in the afternoon or evening? Schedule your study session then. Another method is to study at the same time of day that you will take the test, so that your brain gets used to working on the material at that time and will be ready to focus at test time.

Step 5: Study!

Once you have done all the study preparation, it's time to settle into the actual studying. Sit down, take a few moments to settle your mind so you can focus, and begin to follow your study plan. Don't give in to distractions or let yourself procrastinate. This is your time to prepare so you'll be ready to fearlessly approach the test. Make the most of the time and stay focused.

Of course, you don't want to burn out. If you study too long you may find that you're not retaining the information very well. Take regular study breaks. For example, taking five minutes out of every hour to walk briskly, breathing deeply and swinging your arms, can help your mind stay fresh.

As you get to the end of each chapter or section, it's a good idea to do a quick review. Remind yourself of what you learned and work on any difficult parts. When you feel that you've mastered the material, move on to the next part. At the end of your study session, briefly skim through your notes again.

But while review is helpful, cramming last minute is NOT. If at all possible, work ahead so that you won't need to fit all your study into the last day. Cramming overloads your brain with more information than it can process and retain, and your tired mind may struggle to recall even previously learned information when it is overwhelmed with last-minute study. Also, the urgent nature of cramming and the stress placed on your brain contribute to anxiety. You'll be more likely to go to the test feeling unprepared and having trouble thinking clearly.

So don't cram, and don't stay up late before the test, even just to review your notes at a leisurely pace. Your brain needs rest more than it needs to go over the information again. In fact, plan to finish your studies by noon or early afternoon the day before the test. Give your brain the rest of the day to relax or focus on other things, and get a good night's sleep. Then you will be fresh for the test and better able to recall what you've studied.

Step 6: Take a Practice Test

Many courses offer sample tests, either online or in the study materials. This is an excellent resource to check whether you have mastered the material, as well as to prepare for the test format and environment.

Check the test format ahead of time: the number of questions, the type (multiple choice, free response, etc.), and the time limit. Then create a plan for working through them. For example, if you have 30 minutes to take a 60-question test, your limit is 30 seconds per question. Spend less time on the questions you know well so that you can take more time on the difficult ones.

If you have time to take several practice tests, take the first one open book, with no time limit. Work through the questions at your own pace and make sure you fully understand them. Gradually work up to taking a test under test conditions: sit at a desk with all study materials put away and set a timer. Pace yourself to make sure you finish the test with time to spare and go back to check your answers if you have time.

After each test, check your answers. On the questions you missed, be sure you understand why you missed them. Did you misread the question (tests can use tricky wording)? Did you forget the information? Or was it something you hadn't learned? Go back and study any shaky areas that the practice tests reveal.

Taking these tests not only helps with your grade, but also aids in combating test anxiety. If you're already used to the test conditions, you're less likely to worry about it, and working through tests until you're scoring well gives you a confidence boost. Go through the practice tests until you feel comfortable, and then you can go into the test knowing that you're ready for it.

Test Tips

On test day, you should be confident, knowing that you've prepared well and are ready to answer the questions. But aside from preparation, there are several test day strategies you can employ to maximize your performance.

First, as stated before, get a good night's sleep the night before the test (and for several nights before that, if possible). Go into the test with a fresh, alert mind rather than staying up late to study.

Try not to change too much about your normal routine on the day of the test. It's important to eat a nutritious breakfast, but if you normally don't eat breakfast at all, consider eating just a protein bar. If you're a coffee drinker, go ahead and have your normal coffee. Just make sure you time it so that the caffeine doesn't wear off right in the middle of your test. Avoid sugary beverages, and drink enough water to stay hydrated but not so much that you need a restroom break 10 minutes into the test. If your test isn't first thing in the morning, consider going for a walk or doing a light workout before the test to get your blood flowing.

Allow yourself enough time to get ready, and leave for the test with plenty of time to spare so you won't have the anxiety of scrambling to arrive in time. Another reason to be early is to select a good seat. It's helpful to sit away from doors and windows, which can be distracting. Find a good seat, get out your supplies, and settle your mind before the test begins.

When the test begins, start by going over the instructions carefully, even if you already know what to expect. Make sure you avoid any careless mistakes by following the directions.

Then begin working through the questions, pacing yourself as you've practiced. If you're not sure on an answer, don't spend too much time on it, and don't let it shake your confidence. Either skip it and come back later, or eliminate as many wrong answers as possible and guess among the remaining ones. Don't dwell on these questions as you continue—put them out of your mind and focus on what lies ahead.

Be sure to read all of the answer choices, even if you're sure the first one is the right answer. Sometimes you'll find a better one if you keep reading. But don't second-guess yourself if you do immediately know the answer. Your gut instinct is usually right. Don't let test anxiety rob you of the information you know.

If you have time at the end of the test (and if the test format allows), go back and review your answers. Be cautious about changing any, since your first instinct tends to be correct, but make sure you didn't misread any of the questions or accidentally mark the wrong answer choice. Look over any you skipped and make an educated guess.

At the end, leave the test feeling confident. You've done your best, so don't waste time worrying about your performance or wishing you could change anything. Instead, celebrate the successful completion of this test. And finally, use this test to learn how to deal with anxiety even better next time.

Review Video: Test Anxiety
Visit mometrix.com/academy and enter code: 100340

Important Qualification

Not all anxiety is created equal. If your test anxiety is causing major issues in your life beyond the classroom or testing center, or if you are experiencing troubling physical symptoms related to your anxiety, it may be a sign of a serious physiological or psychological condition. If this sounds like your situation, we strongly encourage you to seek professional help.

Online Resources

Due to our efforts to try to keep this book to a manageable length, we've created a link that will give you access to all of your online resources:

mometrix.com/resources719/terranextg5rl

It's Your Moment, Let's Celebrate It!

Share your story @mometrixtestpreparation